MACK HANAN

ACCELERATED GROWTH PLANNING

Profit Improvement Strategies for Consumer, Industrial, and Service Business Game Plans

McGraw-Hill Book Company

New York St. Louis San Francisco Auckland Bogotá Düsseldorf Johannesburg London Madrid Mexico Montreal New Delhi Panama Paris São Paulo Singapore Sydney Tokyo Toronto

Library of Congress Cataloging in Publication Data

Hanan, Mack.
Accelerated growth planning: profit improvement strategies
for consumer, industrial, and service business
game plans.

Includes index.
1. Corporate planning. 2. Corporate profits.
3. Branded merchandise. I. Title.
HD30.28.H36 658.1'554 77-13201
ISBN 0-07-025971-2

1234567890 FGRFGR 7654321098

The editors for this book were W. Hodson Mogan and Tobia L. Worth, the designer was Elliot Epstein, and the production supervisor was Teresa F. Leaden. It was set in Caledonia by Monotype Composition Company.

Printed and bound by Fairfield Graphics.

To my colleagues
Drs. Arnold Amstutz and Jack Donis,

who have shared their disciplines
with me with such commitment
that I have been able to blend some of
them into my own and who, by doing
so, have accelerated my own growth.

CONTENTS

FOREWORD

All up and down Route 128 in Massachusetts and throughout the Santa Clara Valley in California, there is a malaise that can be described as "darkness at noon." It is a young high-technology company's prolonged stay in the time tunnel between the market entry of a new product line and the coming on-stream of its initial earnings. This malaise is sometimes referred to as the "Route 128 syndrome": overengineer a new product, overcost it, and overinventory it, but undermarket it.

While this syndrome is typical of young high-technology businesses, no industry is immune to it. Some new products, equipment, or systems, in spite of being undermanaged, go on to become branded "big winners." Most never make it. They plateau when they are knocked off by a superior competitor in an industrial version of *Here Comes the Judge*. Or they simply run out of gas a few miles from the barn, penetrating their unenthusiastic markets just far enough beyond breakeven to give their sponsors an irrational hope that they will be more than simply premature commodities. These are the eight-barrel pumpers that oilmen dread. Neither dry holes nor gushers, they always promise but never produce a winner.

How many capital-equipment managers who are stuck in the time tunnel, watching their seed capital run down while they await the first significant sale or the second one that will confirm the first sale as something more than a one-time fluke, know how to accelerate a new product's growth into branded status?

How many managers of prematurely peaked commodities in foods and drugs know how to restore their growth at an accelerated rate?

In both cases, the answer is "Few." However many such managers there may be, their number is certainly no larger than that of the relatively small band of entrepreneurial managers who can dare to question even a big-winning brand's rate of growth and ask "How much higher, how much faster can it go?"

And when the brands degenerate into mature-commodity status, to which all brands must eventually succumb, what then? Where are the managers of all the sober, hardworking companies in the Midwest whose commodity products supply the merchandising machine of Sears, let's say, who can revive selected products by rebranding them into accelerated growers once again as IBM has done with computers and General Foods has done with Jell-O?

The objective of this book is to provide a compendium of thrust strategies for managers and their planners who want to be able to grow new products faster, accelerate the upward momentum of even high-flying brands before competition sticks holes in them, and reposition premature and mature commodities from a half-life into winning status for a second time around. These are the major ways that produce premium profits—the premium profits which enable new enterprises to consolidate their business positions and which provide longer-established businesses with the internally generated capital they require to nourish new enterprises.

Accelerated growth is the key to premium profits: profits that can be earned at twice the rate of growth of the gross national product or more. In turn, premium profits are the key to internal capital formation. Today and for the foreseeable future, any growth strategy worthy of the name must be devoted to supplying capital from operations rather than from debt or equity offerings.

Ever since the 1974–1975 recession, the business environment has constrained the accumulation and conservation of growth capital. Three major developments are largely responsible. The first development is the energy crisis. It ended the ready availability of low-cost fuel. Capital has been flowing outward from every corporate treasury ever since to pay for energy. As the cost of energy resources has risen, growth has slowed. Since every company has a finite amount of human power and capital from which it can grow, this amount dissipates rapidly when it is taxed with a severely multiplied oil price. When a company's real disposable income falls, its consumption spending and investment spending fall with it.

The second development is the realization that there are economic restraints other than energy costs on the ability of innovative technology to produce an endless, or at least a dependable, supply of brandable new commercial products, the kind of products that bring capital into a business. The price of fundamental technical advance, in terms of environmental and public health costs as well as actual money costs, has often become prohibitive. There is also a good deal of evidence to suggest that the output of research and development has been steadily declining in many industries at the same time that cost inflation has been placing a premium on its productivity. In these industries, which include basic industrial manufacturing as well as high technology, inflation is overcoming the capability of technology to improve efficiency. As development and production costs rise, a fair price for many new-technology products cannot be recovered because fair pricing for the maker would unfairly wipe out customer savings in operating costs.

The third new development is the continuing revolution in corporate and personal values. In response, management has had to comply with the demands of increasing legislative intervention in policy and operations. Additionally and often more meaningfully, pressures from quasi-legislative consumer and other interest groups have demanded changes in strategy and even the translation of business objectives into public action. As a result, capital has found still another channel by which to flow outward.

Many companies cut costs as a means of improving capital turnover. Others push sales. But pressing for increased sales volume by itself is no answer. When companies go all out to support higher volume without paying a corresponding regard to profits, heavy inventories are built and new money must often be invested in plant and equipment. Sales might then rise 25 percent, from $16 million to $20 million. Operating profit might go up 10 percent, from $1 million to $1.1 million. Coincidentally, inventories might then rise from $6 million to $8 million, while receivables could go from $2.5 million to as much as $4 million. Operating profit might then drop from 7 percent or so of total capital employed to around 5 percent. When this happens, management finds itself in an uncomfortable position. Growth, defined as volume, has indeed occurred. Profits have grown, too, but not apace. Instead of being able to make an incremental contribution, management must now stand in line, hat in hand, to petition for incremental cash.

It is one thing to say that only profitable growth can generate capital; that statement is hard to contradict. The feat is harder still to pull off. Together with my original fellows here at the Wellspring, Drs. Arnold Amstutz and Jack Donis, we turned (quite logically, we supposed) to the planning process as our chosen instrument for capital generation by means of profit acceleration. Our reward was disenchantment, not confirmation. The traditional planning format was so ill suited, we found, to accelerate profit growth that our conclusion was that "we could not get there from here" with it.

Accordingly, we began to create and counsel on the application of a "capitalized" planning process that could convert growth plans into capital generators. We said that if the planning process was to be made relevant to the needs of most businesses, it had to be able to meet three demands:

1. It must encourage accelerated growth at a pace of 2 or more times the rate of growth of the gross national product.
2. It must generate enough capital to subsidize the financing of new developmental product lines and venture businesses from within along with the rebranding of selected commodity products into big winners.
3. It must be put together in an evergreen type of format that is responsive to swift and significant change so that growth planning, like the management of growth, can be a continuing function instead of a periodic crash program that is obsolete before the ink dries.

Unless these demands are met, our experience has taught us that planning for growth can be a nostalgic reverie, a ritual wafer offered up to top management as a token of goodwill and commendable intentions.

Capitalized planning through accelerated profit growth has become Wellspring gospel. We practice it and preach it. We wish to acknowledge here with thanks the permission we have received to refer to three previous preachments: the outline of a marketcentered organization structure, which first appeared as an article in the *Harvard Business Review;* the examples of venture objectives and acquisition criteria, which appear in the McGraw-Hill book *Venture Management;* and the illustrations of consumer market segmentation, which are adapted from the AMACOM book *Life-Styled Marketing.*

The time when a business could accelerate its growth by opening its doors a little bit earlier every morning in the hope of catching a lucky curve on the way up or by potshotting money at a problem is over and done with. Darkness at noon has a way of lingering on into the night. When the judge comes in the form of a supercompetitor who moves into a sheltered franchise, he can come down hard and with terrible retribution for past assumptions that suddenly no longer prove out. And when a mature commodity that has been the flagship of a market franchise for years, even for decades, finally folds, a whole business can fold with it.

We find salvation only in planning deliberately for accelerated growth and in planning for it with a process that has been specifically engineered for acceleration. We advocate planned acceleration because we have seen firsthand the problems of turning around and rejuvenating a reactionary management that has disdained for too long to generate its own capital. We have also seen the business atrocities and market outrages committed by revolutionary managements that, one morning at 9:01 A.M., have tried to convert their businesses into short-term capital machines. Our recommended course is the substance of this book. Accelerate the growth of new products and brands. Rebrand commodities. Plan to grow incremental profit, not volume or market share. Plan to make capital generation your plan's main job.

MACK HANAN
THE WELLSPRING GROUP, INC.

How to Create Your Own Accelerated Growth Plan

Throughout the book, you will see references to application work sheets called "planning pages." These pages, which are assembled in numerical order at the end of each chapter, are designed for you to use in creating your own accelerated growth plan. When you have filled them out according to the instructions in the text and assembled them with the title pages in Appendix 2, you will have a completed plan.

1

THE BRANDING PRINCIPLE

There are four principal attributes of a branded business or product:

1. It commands premium price.
2. Perceived value exceeds price even though price is premium.
3. Manufacturer and marketer are positioned as adding meaningful value to the user, not to the product.
4. Value-adding positioning rules out debate on the merits of comparative performance benefits.

For the fourth quarter of the twentieth century, management will have to make a new accommodation to growth. Slow and steady growth, which has won a lot of races in its day, is no longer good enough to serve as the universal role model. It is too speedily and too surely overtaken. Rising costs and inflationary erosion of dollar values that nullify profits, preemptive competition that comes unexpectedly from diagonal technologies to knock off a marketing advantage, quantum scientific jumps and laboratory leapfrogs that end-run huge capital investments in older technologies and convert investments in market franchises into sunk costs that can never be returned, compliance with legislative strictures that eliminate in a single stroke the technical or cost basis for a business, in-and-out sources of supply that force recourse to expensive self-manufacture or to the more costly substitution of key ingredients or processes, and a highly mobile market demand that is increasingly sensitive to being influenced not just by its perceptions of value but also by emotional reactions toward its suppliers—all these factors can make slow growth expensive, uncertain, and unable to be self-financing in the long run. Accelerated profit making, striking responsively while an iron is hot and bringing home premium revenues before the economic, competitive, legislative, technical, or marketing environments change, has become the order of the day.

Twentieth-century management will have to become the art of accelerated growth. New products will have to be moved faster than ever up the profit curve. Existing brands, management's most powerful profit producers, will have to be accelerated higher more rapidly and be kept moving upward longer. No longer can commodities simply be consigned to a maintenance type of management that will let the air slowly out of their cost base, market them by deal and discount, and apply only ultraselective marginal alterations as they slip and slide their way down the earnings curve. On a highly specific basis, chosen commodities, especially some premature commodity products that once promised to achieve brand status but have never made it, will have to be repositioned into premium-priced winners that earn the profits from which internal capital formation can occur.

No product line, no product, will be able to escape growth scoping.

Inescapable Growth Acceleration

For many companies—indeed, for almost every well-managed company—accelerated profit growth may be the only way in which significant capital accumulation can take place. These are the companies that are already working in all the accredited, conventional ways to improve their productivity by reducing costs and bettering utilization of their plant operations, labor force, energy consumption, and materials purchasing. They are collecting receivables faster and using credit in more sophisticated ways. They are standardizing products, turning around or divesting marginal operations, stretching out investments, and controlling inventory buildup. Some companies are ingeniously trying to offset some of their compliance costs. In the area of environmental protection, for example, they are squeezing out a small return on their investment from the capture and sale of residual materials, the recycling of control agents, or the marketing of their consultation services in pollution control to companies with similar problems or processes.

For every step forward they take, however, most of these companies find themselves beset by new and costly reasons why it is difficult to accumulate capital: competition maintains pressure against price increases, costs of purchased materials and services continue to rise, labor costs keep pace with increased costs of living, interest rates on borrowed funds remain high, compliance costs escalate, and additional revenue potential is often lost in the translation of foreign currencies. Like Alice in Wonderland, they are running faster and faster just to stay in place.

We do not scorn or disparage traditional strategies of capital management. We like to think of them as standard operating procedures. A compendium of capital management strategies appears in Appendix 1. If you are not using these strategies, you should be; if you are already using them, they are probably not good enough by themselves. In the long run, there is no salvation in saving capital. You cannot save your way to the ever-improving profit you need in order to grow a business in the 1970–1980 environment. Sooner or later (we favor sooner) the revenue-producing process must be accelerated. New products must be branded. Commodities must be rebranded. Brands must be perpetuated by means of thrusted growth strategies.

Undeniable Growth-planning Platitudes

Everybody talks about growth. Many of us are platitudinous about it. One reasonably infallible way of going about accelerating the growth process is to adapt three basic injunctions of the song "Accentuate the Positive" to managing a business:

> "Accentuate the positive" by concentrating on selling your big-winner products to your heavy-profit-contributor markets.
>
> "Eliminate the negative" by bringing profit-detracting products to break-even or by divesting them through withdrawal and write-off at net book values, along with eliminating marginal markets.
>
> "Don't mess with Mr. In-Between" by screening out product lines or candidates that cannot meet minimum financial growth criteria.

Some platitudes are more robust than others. A half dozen in which it may pay to put some faith are these:

1. When everybody approves an accelerated growth plan, it is probably too conservative.
2. The actual "worst case" is always 10 percent below your worst-case expectation.
3. A dollar saved in reducing the cost of a strategy will depreciate rapidly.
4. Every time a trade-off between two strategies is made, somebody will be wrong.
5. Get out of your losers and let your winners run.
6. All growth is temporary.

When we have to put our money where our mouth is, however, we go to the wall with the *branding principle.* It is more difficult to execute than the platitudes and is just as undeniable.

The Branding Principle

Branding is the key to accelerated growth. Branded businesses and products are premium earners of growth profits because they and they alone can command premium price. Our definition of a brand is based on this unique distinction: *a brand is a commander of premium price.* Growth businesses are businesses that have one or more *price commanders* in their mix.

Branding to us is not merely naming a product or trademarking it with the maker's signature or seal. That would be too easy. After all, many commodities are called by name. A brand, defined in capital-generating terms, is a product whose perceived value is noncompetitive. So superior is its perceived benefit that no competitive product or business can match its value in use.

It is an understatement to say that a brand's perceived premium value *justifies* a premium price. In reality, a brand's perceived premium value *requires* a premium price; or, as we like to say, it *commands* price.

To equip a business to be a price commander, its products must be perceived by its market to offer an unsurpassed value. The genesis of branding lies in this perception. To grow a business at an accelerated rate, therefore, it must be brought to branded status as quickly as possible and held there in command of a premium price as long as possible. This guarantees its contribution of premium profits. Brand building has two basic rules: (1) Take off fast and high. (2) Stay high long. Everything we do with new products, existing brands, and prematurely fallen commodities is designed to achieve brand status. When we encounter a mature commodity that can be turned around, we try to reposition it to brandedness. If we can help rebrand it, we can gain the pricing leverage that will make it a big winner of profits once again.

Price command opens the door to market leadership. It also permits the competitive isolation of a business. Rivals who try to erode the business's franchise by price cutting run the risk of reducing their own profit on sales. They also may underscore the price commander's superior perceived value by their contrast. In effect, they act unwittingly to validate the brand's claim to preemptive value. They tend to make commodities of each other, often leaving the price commander in sole possession of the market perception of preempted value.

The W. T. Grant Model of Negative Growth

There is no single model for accelerated growth based on brandedness. But there is a tried and true model, it seems, of accelerated negative growth. Exhibit 1-1 signals some of its predictable highlight events. Not every scenario of negative growth follows this sequencing. Yet so many do that it is instructive to illuminate one of them, the W. T. Grant model, as a fair representation of what not to do.

In 1965, Grant had sales of somewhat under $1 billion and net earnings of $30 million. By 1975, sales had risen to almost $1,750 billion, with negative net earnings representing a loss of more than $150 million. Grant, like many other retailers, undertook a large-scale capital expansion in the mid-1960s. At first, profits kept pace. Then Grant stopped planning for capital generation. From 1963 to 1973, Grant opened more than 600 new large stores and enlarged almost 100 others. Staffing and managing them placed a great strain on the company's management capability. At some point, recruitment and training could no longer keep up. Mediocrity began to show.

Even worse, Grant's positioning became vague. No one could decide what kind of business it was. As a result, Grant took a position midway between the discounters on the one hand and Sears, Montgomery Ward, and J. C. Penney on the other. This turned out to be an unbrandable stance.

As befits a midway positioning, merchandise selection was broadened to have something on hand for everybody. Soon inventory problems could not be coped with. With hindsight, it was concluded: "We were selling stale merchandise in our new stores, and the company was reluctant to move in and take the necessary steps to balance inventory by the use of markdowns." Before the merchandise could be moved off the shelves, seasons and taste in styles had changed. "We had so much stuff just sitting there that we couldn't free up the dollars to do a good seasonal merchandising job." Classic errors occurred. A conscious effort was made to trade up in a branded manner, but it lacked the consistency of a planned progression. Several price ranges were jumped at once. Customers no longer knew what to expect.

Toward the end, Grant began a heavy credit promotion in an attempt to move merchandise, especially big-ticket items such as television sets, major appliances, and power tools. All of them were branded with Grant's own label, which had never established consumer acceptance. If the market would not give Grant a branded acceptance, Grant would give the market credit. "We went into credit in a big way to get the new stores rolling, but there were few restrictions . . . so we ended up with a disastrous credit operation with excessive charge-offs and bad debts."

What went wrong with Grant? In many respects, this is a typical case of a once-branded supplier permitting its brand to fall into commodity positioning and then attempting to make up in size proliferation and sales volume what had been lost in premium profit making. It is also typical that these high crimes and misdemeanors of management were committed in the guise of growth. Under a true accelerated growth thrust that would set profit objectives instead of mass goals and that would plan for Grant's rebranding, even as late as the early 1970s it would have been possible for Grant to change direction by adopting rebranding strategies such as these:

1. *Establish a growth business position.* Use advertising to establish market acceptance for house brands.

2. *Adopt an entrepreneurial management style.* Train and motivate a high-producing management.

3. *Target the heavy-profit-contributor market.* Go after the same target market as discounters K Mart and Woolco. Gear merchandise to target-market price points.

4. *Pair big winner products with the market.* Return to the brandable types of merchandise that originally built Grant's reputation.

5. *Manage cash flow and pricing strategies.* Get out of the big-ticket commodity items that account for high sales revenues but not many customers. Take markdowns to regain a good open-to-buy situation. Stock fresh new merchandise, and re-establish liquid inventory positions at the local-store level. Curtail or end credit operations.

6. *Use turnaround and divestment strategies.* Get down to a smaller number of profitable stores by turning some losers around and closing or subleasing others.

Grant's experience symbolizes the unforgiving nature of today's business environment. When growth lags or becomes negative, therapy is difficult and expensive and has a high likelihood of being unsuccessful. Risk is no longer single. It has become an amalgam of several dynamic factors: a newly exaggerated fickleness in the economy, new legislative constraints, new competition from diagonal technologies and not merely from adjacent firms in the same industry, swift swings in market preferences, rising energy costs, and difficulties in obtaining dependable supplies of outside capital. Yet by far the heaviest element of risk is found in failing to accelerate growth in a branded manner.

Brand Country/Commodity Country Interfaces

In most companies, the 80:20 rule governs the distribution of brands and commodities in the marketing mix. Up to 80 percent of profitable sales volume may come from as little as 20 percent or so of all products in the mix. These are largely the branded products that command premium price. The remaining 20 percent of profitable sales volume comes from the 80 percent of products in the mix that usually are commodities.

Commodities are bought and sold in what we call "Commodity Country" in Exhibit 1-2. Commodity products are "bought" far more often than

EXHIBIT 1-1

PROBLEM-REACTION SCENARIO

Growth-induced problems	*Negative-growth Management reactions*
1. High-multiple growth objectives are set, and prolific resource allocation is authorized to achieve them.	1. Products, markets, management staff, and functional organization proliferate.
2. Management communication becomes bogged down.	2. Commonality of original growth objectives thins out, and information exchange is short-circuited.
3. Sensitivity diminishes to the nature of changing market needs or to the reaction time required to meet them.	3. Product mix becomes cost-ineffective, incorrect priorities are assigned to R&D, and out-of-stock or overinventoried positions reduce some sales and add to many costs.
4. Brands decline into commodities.	4. Customers defect, trade reactions turn negative, and management talks of better days ahead while sales force morale declines under relentless price competition.
5. Market share shrinks.	5. As margins diminish, price reductions further reduce revenues in the attempt to regain market share while promotion costs rise.
6. Sales costs increase while profits on sales fall.	6. Overcentralization of control functions results in loss of local-management autonomy.
7. Management becomes confused, disharmonious, and disoriented by an identity crisis.	7. A power struggle occurs, causing misdirection of top-level attention and energy. If the business is lucky, a new dedication is made to accelerated growth. Otherwise, the business may be acquired or required to foreclose.

EXHIBIT 1-2

BRAND COUNTRY/COMMODITY COUNTRY SALES INTERFACES

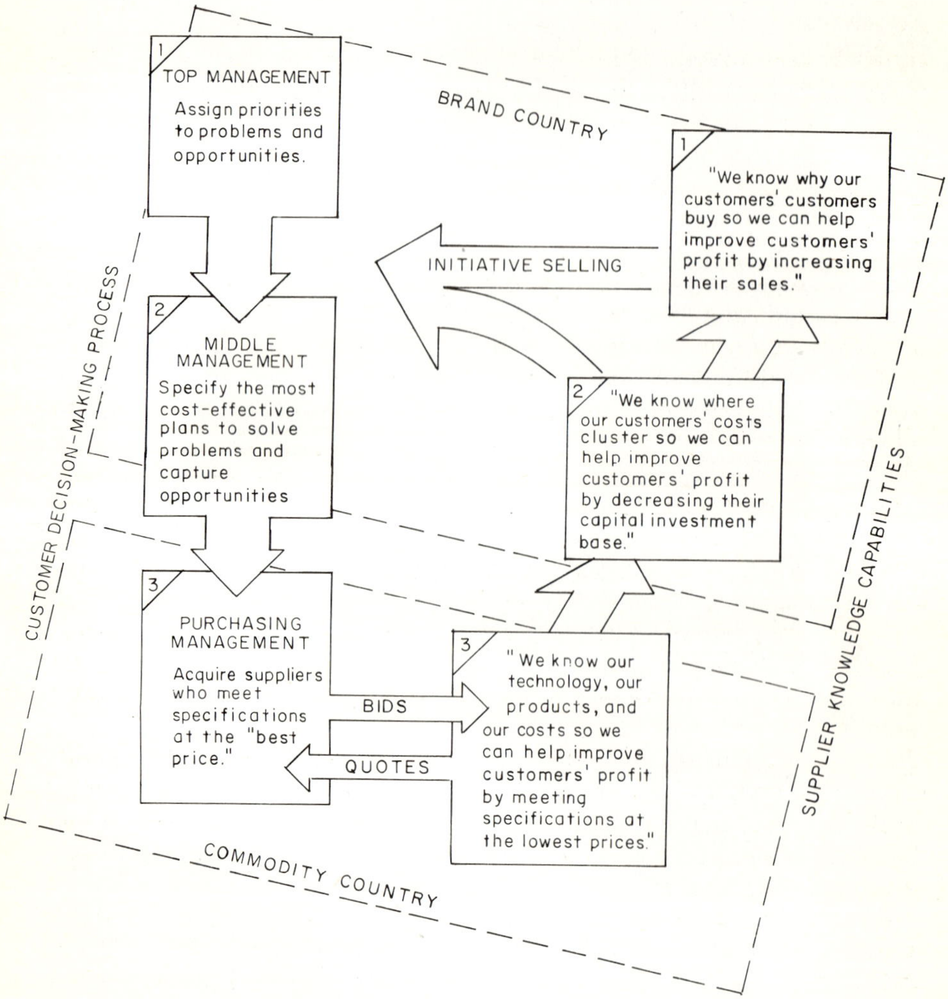

they are "sold." That is, the initiative is taken by a customer who aggressively solicits bids from optional suppliers. In turn, suppliers react with quotations. This is not to say that commodity suppliers are passive—far from it, as their cost of sales generally testifies. But the difference between being an actively reactive supplier and an active initiator of sales opportunities is one of the major differences between commodity sellers and brand marketers.

Brand suppliers are positioned as initiators, and commodity suppliers are positioned as reactors to the typical customer decision-making process shown in Exhibit 1-2. At Level 1, the level of top management, the focus is on assigning priorities to the problems that confront the business. Products and services are meaningless at this level. Only solutions to priority problems are meaningful. Top management passes its priorities down to Level 2, where middle management must specify the most cost-effective solutions to these problems. Middle management's specifications take the form of recommendations that usually are presented for top-management approval as plans. In the same way that priorities are the products of top management, plans for the solution of priority problems or the capitalizing of priority opportunities are the products of middle management.

When middle management's specifications for solving priority problems are accepted by top management—this means, in dollar terms, that a budget has been allocated—the purchasing teams of management that function at Level 3 come into play. They set out to acquire bids from alternate suppliers of product components in the approved solutions. These bids seek two qualifications on the part of every supplier: (1) Specifications must be met. (2) Price must be the "best price," which means the buyer's price.

A customer's Level 3 interacts with a supplier's Level 3 in Commodity Country. To deal in Commodity Country, a supplier must have three knowledge capabilities. A supplier must be able to say: "We know our technology, we know the products it yields in terms of their physical and chemical properties and their performance benefits that permit specifications to be met, and we know our costs so that we can peg the best price as close to cost as possible." This interface between a customer's Level 3 decision makers and a supplier's Level 3 knowledge capability is the universal shopping mall for commodity products.

Brands, on the other hand, are not transacted in this 3:3 fashion. Branded products and many rebranded commodities move on the first and second levels of the customer-decision-maker/supplier-knowledge interface. This is "Brand Country" in Exhibit 1-2. Brand suppliers deal actively in solutions to priority problems at Level 2. They also help assign priorities to management problems at Level 1.

A supplier's tickets of admission to Brand Country are very different from the credentials that confer bid-list status at the 3:3 levels. In Brand

Country, the premium is on knowledge of a customer's business. This knowledge lies outside the supplier's corporate frame of reference, far transcending the internal knowledge of technology, product performance, and cost that are the tools of the trade in Commodity Country. To sell brands, a supplier must extend the boundaries of marketing awareness to include a knowledge of customer cost clusters so that these can be decreased by a branded solution. Even beyond a customer's costs, a supplier must raise consciousness to the needs of a customer's customers so that opportunities for new sales revenues for all three—customer, customer's customers, and supplier—can be gained and profits mutually improved.

Where you sell in Exhibit 1-2 generally determines what you sell. Only commodities, never brands, are transacted at Level 3. In our own shorthand jargon, we call commodities "3:3 products." Only brands and rebranded commodities are transacted at Levels 1 and 2. Occasionally a rebranded commodity is sold at Level 3 because of a customer's traditional buying procedures or a supplier's traditional selling policies and practices. But it will still command a premium price in recognition of its branded status.

The message of Exhibit 1-2 is clear. To brand or rebrand a product, you must position it as a superior cost-effective solution to a primary customer problem. The solution, not the product, must be sold. The more uniquely cost-effective your solution is in comparison with competitive solutions, the stronger your branded position will be and the higher premium your price can bear because the greater your product's perceived value will be. If perceived value is high enough, you will be able to rule out debate on the merits of a branded product's comparative performance benefits. The perception of premium value added to the user will replace an examination of the values added to product performance.

Brand Doctrine: How Brands Are Made

Companies that have an above-average track record in making brands are either discoverers or imitators of a regular, persistent method that has become policy. Brand builders make brands because they see this as their business. Many of them have expressed their policy in the form of a doctrine. The doctrine generally encompasses three interrelated parts. One part seeks agreement on the purpose of brands so that their vital contribution to growth profits is clearly understood and accepted. A second part sets guidelines for the premium pricing of brands, which is their chief instrument for earning premium profits. The third part underscores the irreplaceable role of marketing in the commercialization of brands.

Brand-building companies disseminate brand doctrine far and wide in their organizations, not only to the marketing functions but also to research and engineering, manufacturing, and finance. The emphasis on creating a superior value/price relationship in a branded product is imbued companywide. Product performance reflects it. So do pricing and promotional positioning. These companies work on the theory that either brand building will be everybody's business or it will be nobody's business.

A generalized brand-building doctrine is shown in Exhibit 1-3.

The Concept of Perceived Value

When we define a brand's power or, for that matter, the power of a rebranded commodity as being derived from its *perceived value,* we are acknowledging the market genesis of branding. The perception of a product or a service as a brand originates in its market. While perceived value is sometimes directly correlated with manufactured or engineered value on a 1:1 basis, it often is not related to them. If you build a better mousetrap and that is all you do, it may not make any difference. Perceived value is based on value in use, not on value in the product. It is independent of the costs or technologies put into a product. Perceived value is dependent only on the benefits that can be contrived from the product. To the extent that these benefits are closely proportional to their developmental, engineered, manufactured, and marketed costs, the product can be said to be cost-effective.

The litmus test for perceived value is price. Markets pay for value. If high value is not perceived, a high price will not be paid. Price is therefore directly proportional to perceived value. The basis for premium price is what the market's perception of value will bear.

Growth planning is the process of building high values into the perceptions of markets. There are times when this will require that added performance values be built into a product. There are other times when added values must be built into a product's sales or marketing approach while the physical product itself remains intact and unaffected. No matter what does or does not happen to the product, the marketing function must always have value added to it if the perceptions of a market are to be engaged. This is the purpose of marketing: to create the basis for a market's perception of preemptive value.

For this reason, most straightforward commodity-product manufacturers do not need a marketing function. Commodities cannot be marketed as long as they remain positioned as commodities, that is, as long as they cannot create the basis for a market's perception of preemptive value. Frank commodities can only be bought and sold, not marketed. Their selling points are the familiar ones of best price, compliance with specifications, and some sort of sweetener for the deal. It is only when a commodity has been rebranded that it can be marketed.

EXHIBIT 1-3

BRAND DOCTRINE

1. The four basic areas of agreement on brand purpose

1.1. The principal objective of a business is to grow incremental profit.

1.2. The principal reason for growing incremental profit is to be self-financing in capital generation.

1.3. The principal means of growing incremental profit is to command premium price.

1.4. Therefore, the principal task of management is to create businesses that can command premium price. These businesses are called branded or specialty, proprietary, or performance businesses.

2. The four guidelines to brand pricing

2.1. The basis for a brand's command of premium price is its market's perception of premium value. A brand's value/price ratio must always favor value.

2.2. A brand's price is based on added value to the user, not added value to the product. This added user value can be computed as a positive return on investment in acquiring the brand.

2.3. When brand price is compared with the return on investment that is represented by price, the brand's value exceeds its price.

2.4. A bargain is a purchase whose value exceeds its price. By this definition, brands are premium-priced bargains. Their premium value exceeds their premium price.

3. The five roles of marketing for brands

3.1. Marketing is the principal brand-building function of a business. Marketing is the only function that can create the perception of added value to the user in a market.

3.2. The principal knowledge capability of a brand-marketing function must be knowledge of the user values that can be added to. There are two main user values that brands add to: (*a*) an improvement in reducing costs and (*b*) an improvement in increasing sales revenues.

3.3. By adding a contribution to reduced cost or increased sales revenue, brands improve customer profit. Profit improvement, which is the means of improving return on investment, is the ultimate user value to be added to by a brand.

3.4. The marketing of branded products is a win-win function: the market wins improved profit by gaining access to premium value, and the marketer wins improved profit by gaining command of premium price.

3.5. Marketing branded products requires going out of business as product supplier. A brand marketer must reenter business as a customer profit improver. For example, a scale manufacturer must go out of business as a product supplier and reenter business as an improver of customer profit by reducing the costs of customer weighing and measuring processes and by improving the contribution of these processes to customer sales revenues.

Marketing is the principal branding function because it is the sole corporate mission with the capability of creating preemptive perceived value. True enough, the value must be in the product before it can be perceived. But value is often present in many products without ever being perceived. Conversely, genuinely superior value is not always present in many other products, and yet a preemptive value of some sort is nonetheless perceived. How does preemptive value enter the perceptions of a market? In every case, marketing puts it there.

For a market, perceiving is believing. If a market perceives preemptive value in a product, the belief is that it is there. The converse is also true. Many premature commodities suffer from disbelief in their preemptive value. Many mature commodities can be rebranded if market belief in a regenerated preemptive value can be fostered.

The great majority of manufacturers excel in building physical value into their products. Few excel in marketing "use value." This is the primary constraint on the accelerated growth of most businesses. Their markets, like all markets, are expert in perceiving value. After all, that is what markets do all day, day in and day out. Yet manufacturers remain inexpert in marketing perceived value to them. This inequality of skill and the lack of common purpose between manufacturers and their markets that it signifies account for a sizable number of new-product failures, short-lived brands, premature commodities, and mature commodities that fail to establish a branded repositioning.

We approach the acceleration of growth by reminding ourselves that growth is completely dependent on premium profits. When we ask ourselves where premium profits are to be found, we locate them within markets. Our growth platform begins when we recall that all profits initially reside in markets. Growing a business at an accelerated rate means capturing more of these profits faster. What kind of trade-off can we offer a market in return? The answer we give ourselves is always the same: a preemptive perceived value or, in business terms, a branded benefit.

When we help develop new products, we act as spokespersons for the preemptive values that their markets must be able to perceive in them when they are commercialized. When we help existing brands enlarge their market penetration, we act as translators of their preemptive value into the perceptions of the new market segments being penetrated. And when we help turn around commodity products, we act as artificial inseminators of preemptive value into the perceptions of their traditional markets. Otherwise, many manufacturers would overengineer production values whose costs would be unrecoverable because they exceed use value. Or they would engineer incorrect production values that do not yield a market's preferred use values. They might also be unsuccessful in marketing the proper values that do exist.

A brand, then, can be defined as a premium use value that is perceived to be preemptive. A rebranded commodity can be defined as a standardized use value that is newly perceived as preemptive. These are the sources for the two basic strategies of accelerated growth planning.

Ruling Out Debate on the Merits

Debate on the relative merits of competitive products is the bane of commodity existence. Ingredients, components, construction features, performance standards and operating benefits, deals and discounts, service, and even a product's bells, whistles, and flags are routinely opened for buyer scrutiny in the hope that some marginal advantage that can justify the maintenance of price will be discerned. Products that are feature-stripped and searched are, by definition, commodities. Brands are immune. How do brands rule out debate on the merits? The answer is straightforward: brands are never marketed on the basis of their merits, so they can never be compared according to them. Brands are marketed in line with the values they add to their users, not the values that have been added to their products. A user value that is perceived to be superior cannot be field-stripped for comparison with other perceptions of value.

A brand that is marketed on the basis of its individual merits is inviting its users to bring it down to commodity status.

The Lincoln-Cadillac case is an excellent example. Throughout many of the years of the 1960 decade, Cadillac outsold Lincoln by 6 or 7 to 1. Did this mean that Cadillac was 6 or 7 times technically superior? Automotive experts have said it was not. In fact, some of them have said that Lincoln was often the superior automobile in terms of construction and performance characteristics. How then did Cadillac outsell Lincoln? Lincoln's analysis is short and sweet. "Lincoln added superior value to its car. Cadillac adds superior value to the user."

So significant was this added user value that General Motors could say without effective challenge: "Cadillac is one of the few material possessions for which there is no true substitute." This reduced Lincoln to an untrue substitute, or a true nonsubstitute, for Cadillac. The validation of Cadillac's claim to brandedness was the inexorable criterion of return on the user's investment. Cadillac owners received greater trade-in value for their cars than Lincoln owners. Given the tangible superiority in resale dollars for a Cadillac, how much incentive was there for buyers of American-made fine cars to debate the merits of Cadillac construction and performance characteristics compared with Lincoln's? The return on investment said it all. It was the embodiment of superior perceived value.

Merits, which is another way of saying values added to a product, are for hagglers to debate in the commodity bazaar in order to play one merit off against another and thereby bring down price. Brands rise above debate. If they fall into it, they become commodities. To remain free from merit-by-merit evaluation of their innards, they must always direct their added values outward to the perceptions of their markets. These perceptions, and nothing else, can keep them protected from debate.

"Bargaining" a Product

In customer language, a product whose perceived value exceeds its price, no matter how high the price may be, is called a "bargain." Accelerated growth is the process of manufacturing and marketing high-priced bargains—not low-priced bargains, which may not sell because their price will not document their premium value or, if they do sell, may not return growth profits; not high-priced nonbargains, which can be politely designated as inventory and less politely described as scrap; but high-priced bargains, the single most difficult achievement of business management and the absolute prerequisite for internal capital generation.

There are relatively few manufacturers and marketers of brands as we define them that we can take as models of growth acceleration. A familiar litany of names comes to mind almost by rote: IBM for data processors, Xerox for copiers, Polaroid and Kodak for cameras, Bayer for aspirin, Johnson & Johnson for health aids, Tampax for feminine-hygiene products, Lubrizol for chemical additives, General Motors for Cadillac. We say "relatively few," because even a complete list would be paltry when compared with the *Fortune* 500 companies that are so rich in commodity earnings that their lack of branded big winners may be obscured. The history of many of these companies shows a gross ineptitude in brand creation and acceleration or, even worse, a track record of premature descent for their brandable products into commodity classification.

Some of these companies have forgotten what they once knew so well, which is what made them great in the first place: the *reductio ad absurdum* of accelerated growth that can be simply stated in this way:

1. Growth comes from premium profits.
2. Premium profits come from premium prices.
3. Premium prices come from brands.
4. Growth comes from brands.

Growth management is brand management. The branding of a business and its products is management's prime task if growth capital is to be generated internally in sufficient amounts to permit the business to expand at least twice as fast as the gross national product.

The Real Task: Branding a Market

It is probably self-serving to our entrepreneurial ego needs to believe that what we do can be called "branding products." We like to think of it this way because it gives us power: it imputes a capability to master our marketing destiny in an always-uncertain business environment. But, in reality, we believe that just as only markets can brand a product, it is equally true that we can put brands only on markets and not on products.

What does it mean to "brand a market," that is, to put our brand on it? It means that we have positioned our product benefit as a bargain in the value perceptions of the market. We have imprinted on the market's collective mind the primacy of our ability to add unusual worth. We have identified the market as *ours*.

A branded market segment bears our label. Temporarily, and generally only for a short time, we can be said to own it. Of course, we never really acquire ownership. The market is always up for grabs. The sole instrument of control that we can have over a market is the delivery of the perception of unique added value.

Part of this perception, naturally enough, is delivered by our products. But by far the larger part is communicated by the marketing function for our product. *Marketing brands markets.* The role of marketing in the branding process can now be seen as the key market maker for brands, creating the predisposition to prefer a branded product on the basis of its value-adding capability which always exceeds its price.

The "Mean Time" Tests of Brand-building Skill

While there are many ways of evaluating management skill, one of the most relevant measures is the brand-building test: how well does management *brand?* A point of view can be taken, and held, that management's principal function of creating added values for its shareholders is best served when products of perceived premium value—and therefore premium price—are developed and maintained: in other words, when management's brand-building skills are the prime source of corporate capital generation.

There are two tests of brand-building skill that use the mean time concept. One is a test of how well brand development time is managed. The other is a test of how well a brand's commercial time in the market is managed.

Mean Time between Brands

A company's management is managing best when the mean time between the development of successive brands is least. A steady brand stream gives management the highest marks. It shows that management has its priorities straight, that resources are being allocated where the profits are, and that revenues and earnings are being periodically refreshed by new sources of income.

Mean Time before Commodity Status

A company's management is managing best when the mean time between the establishment of brand status for a product and its decline into commodity status is longest. A long holding time for brands to command premium price enables the brand to pay back its original investment, accumulate maximum profits, and help pay for inevitable failures of other members of the product family. Mean time before descent into commodity status is a true test of marketing skill. Marketing is what keeps a brand up or allows its decline to be managed at the slowest rate of dropoff and with the preservation of the highest margins on the way down.

Taken together, these two mean-time concepts can be summarized in this way: How good is a management's brand-building skill? It rates high when two conditions are met: *Brand development time is short; brand maintenance time is long.*

Strategy Thrust Systems

We believe that accelerated growth planning, like business strategy planning in general, must be segmented and custom-tailored to each type of product and business segment. The growth of new products and existing brands requires a system of strategy thrusts that is very different from the rebranded growth of commodities. There is little to choose from in terms of degree of difficulty. The odds prove that it is extremely difficult to generate new brands and to accelerate the upward thrust of already-branded products. We accept this as a given. On the other hand, it is equally challenging to rebrand a commodity. The central issue is not difficulty: it is difference. The strategy options are different. The management style must be different, too.

To accelerate the growth of new products and brands, we recommend a brand-building thrust system composed of up to six strategy options. These options are the building blocks of branding. They are designed, first and foremost, to help you establish a defensible branded position for a business by pairing its product benefits with the needs of the product's heavy-profit-contributor market and also by aligning the values of the business with market values. Other strategy options will help you center your brand's business organization structure in its heavy-profit-contributor market, apply premium pricing to the brand, create high-awareness/positive-attitude advertising for it, and eventually proliferate a brand family of related products from your original offering.

The strategy mix for accelerating the growth of commodities by means of rebranding thrusts presents a more complicated set of options. This suggests that rebranding can require a more concerted attack on a market's perceptions than entering a new brand candidate or accelerating the growth of an existing brand. This is so. A commodity becomes a commodity for valid reasons. These reasons must be counteracted. To overcome them will demand a consideration of such options as product repositioning for turnaround, marketcentering the sales organization, selling in a consultative manner that shows customers how to improve their profit by using the commodity product, either alone or coordinated with other products and services in a system, applying systems pricing, creating profit-improving advertising, and integrating the business in a vertical organization structure with related businesses.

These are the basic strategy thrusts that we will work with to plan accelerated growth through the branding principle. In the first part of this book, we will help you to preplan, that is, to bedrock your growth base. We recommend four ways of laying the growth foundation. One is to adopt entrepreneurial management strategies and construct growth teams to use them. Another is to consolidate the management systems that must support growth planning. A third is to target prime growth markets and make what we call fair assumptions about the impact of relevant variables on their growth. The fourth is to categorize growth sources and set objectives.

When you have preplanned in these ways, you will be ready to accelerate growth in keeping with the guidelines we will suggest.

PART ONE
PREPLANNING

2

BEDROCKING THE GROWTH BASE

There are four preplanning strategies for bedrocking the growth base:

1. Entrepreneurial growth management and growth team construction
2. Growth systems consolidation
3. Growth market targeting and fair assumptions about market growth
4. Growth source categorization and growth objective setting

2-1 ENTREPRENEURIAL GROWTH MANAGEMENT AND GROWTH TEAM CONSTRUCTION

Entrepreneurial management makes growth. Markets are the genesis of growth, but entrepreneurial managers make it. Three attributes characterize entrepreneurial style. Without them growth prospects range from unlikely to impossible. The first style characteristic is a clear, sharp business positioning. The business is readily identifiable from competition. Second in the hierarchy of objectives is profit dominance. The thrust for profit pervades the entire business. The third characteristic is functional concentration embodied in the manager's growth team.

Commercial Integrity

An entrepreneurial management style maximizes growth potential by emphasizing a clear-cut, sharply held business positioning. The business image has commercial integrity: it holds together as a unit that stands for something preemptive in the way of benefiting its customers. It communicates a single purpose, giving it a pointed identity. Concentration is the core of growth. Consistency in communication of the concentrated image of the business is the multiplier of growth.

By concentrating on a single business purpose, heavy profit contributors are relieved of doubt about the kind of business they are dealing with. The know at all times that "*this business* is the one that" provides the preemptive benefit they prefer.

Use a separate copy of Planning Page 1 to create a concentrated positioning statement for every brand-building and commodity-rebranding thrust. At the same time, create positions for the major products involved.

Profit Dominance

In a growth business, profit is the controlling objective. Other objectives such as sales volume and market share are subservient to their profit contribution. The dominance of profit in entrepreneurial management style is acknowledged by the rank order of objectives on Planning Page 2. Use a separate copy of the planning page to scope your objectives in approximate "soft numbers" for every brand-building or rebranding strategy thrust.

Functional Concentration

Growth style requires concentration on the smallest number of functions that can make the greatest contribution to accelerated profit making. The type and number of functions vary with different industries, but three central functions in every growth business are information resourcing and market research, sales, and finance. Product development or R&D may also play a prime role if new-product businesses or venture enterprises are involved.

Use a separate copy of Planning Page 3 to staff and budget the functions you will concentrate on for every brand-building or rebranding strategy thrust.

2-2 GROWTH SYSTEMS CONSOLIDATION

The penalty for growth in good times is often "functional fractionalization." Management functions become atomized, swelling in size and acquiring an independent life in more or less splendid isolation from other related functions. Communication and coordination suffer. The penalty for fractionalization is the impediment of growth. Decisions that must be made jointly are made separately. Surprises, generally unpleasant ones, occur. Confusion, disharmony, and the costs of doing business proliferate. As a result, capital resources are badly used.

By adopting a systems approach, you can consolidate related functions at a lower operating cost for their combined activities and with considerably improved effectiveness.

Three corporate or divisional systems can generally be put together from the typical hodgepodge of separate yet interdependent functions: a consultation and control system, a profit prediction and projection system, and a planning and information system. Each system should be organized on a market basis. To make certain that these systems are taken seriously, they should be formally structured and integrated into the organization chart as permanent staff services.

Consultation and Control System

Top corporate and division management consults on three major functions. One is finance, in which management controls the sources and distribution of funds. The second is market research, by which management controls its understanding of customer dynamics. The third is technology, with which management controls its basic processing capabilities and their application by research and development in the area of pure science and by product development.

When these three functions remain fractionalized, technology is unguided by the priorities of market needs. It often builds to the wrong end uses—wrong in the sense that they turn out to be unmarketable or unprofitable to market. Finance, for its part, is cut off from the kind of intimate knowledge it needs about technical or market development costs. Because a reasonably accurate cost base is missing from its inputs, it generates incorrect profit predictions. Sometimes it never even gets that far. Without knowing costs and probable contributions, finance must allocate development funds on a flimsy best-guess basis, duplicating technology's blind stab at estimating market needs. Market research fails to test acceptance for realistic value/price ratios because neither finance nor technology communicates with it.

These three functions can be made to contribute to growth by systemizing them into a single management unit along the lines of Exhibit 2-1. Under this type of unified direction, you can help assure that market need priorities are made known to technology, that the proper brand-building and commodity-rebranding projects are adequately funded, and that the price, cost, and volume interrelationships of market penetration are profitably proportioned.

If you elect to organize a consolidated control and consultation system, use a separate copy of Planning Page 4 to work out its agenda for every market segment it will serve.

Profit Prediction and Projection System

A second consolidated management system is composed of representatives of finance, marketing and sales, and technology who come together to predict the most probable profit outcomes of various brand-building or commodity-rebranding strategies and to project them over a 3-year time frame.

The end objective of this system is to display potential bottom-line futures for a company or division under a full range of outside conditions that can make an impact on it and the acceptable responses it can make to them. As each future is displayed, management has the opportunity to evaluate its attractiveness. Management can say, "That is an attractive future. How can we achieve it?" or "That's not where we want to come out. How can we avoid it?"

Exhibit 2-2 shows the interactions between finance, sales and marketing, and technical services within a profit prediction and projection system. Sales and marketing generate an ongoing supply of brand building and commodity-rebranding strategy options. What if we launch this new product? Will it be brandable if we price it at this point? What if we concentrate our resources on rebranding this commodity and reduce support for the rest of the line? What if we apply this brand penetration strategy to this market but not that one? Finance can then respond with pro forma roll-outs of the most likely profit outcomes for every strategy option. Technical provides the cost/volume information required by finance and fertilizes sales and marketing with the end-use benefits that its capabilities can deliver so that they can be matched against market needs.

If you elect to organize a consolidated profit prediction and projection system, use a separate copy of Planning Page 5 to work out its agenda for every market segment it will serve.

Planning and Information System

Information gathering and assessment, and subsequent use of the information as the basis for growth planning, are two sides of the same coin. As a result of consolidating these two functions into a single planning and information system, each function can make a necessary contribution to the other. Growth planning can make certain that it has the required fact base to work with. Information can make certain that growth plans fully utilize its knowledge resources, building soundly on its assessments and giving adequate advance notice of upcoming needs to know.

The combined output of a planning and information system takes the form of strategy options made ready for management deliberation and selection. The options are best generated by a market model that simulates the real world of the marketplace as if it were the marketplace itself. For this reason, it is referred to as an "as if" model. Against its values, a multiple of "what if" questions can be asked: What if we were to market a new brand candidate of this or that configuration? What if a major competitor were to seek high-velocity market penetration for a rebranded commodity while we react by lowering the price of our parity product? This type of simulation system can provoke much useful trial-and-error decision making on a continuing schedule, bringing with it the added advantage of allowing strategy gaming to take place in economical privacy rather than in the real and expensive world of the marketplace.

A market model of this type, which can also be called a "demand model," does not need to be highly sophisticated or computerized to be useful. The principal requirement is that it represent a quantification of the values held by a market which influence its purchase decisions. These values should be "read" like this: *The market places a value of* X *on making this decision in this manner under these conditions. If the conditions are changed in this way, what change, if any, will the market make in its values?*

Market values can best be perceived by reference to two guides. One is the price that the market is willing to pay. The higher the price, the greater the value that the market holds for a given product. The other guide is market share. The higher the share, the greater the value held by the market in doing business with a given supplier. Where high price and high share coincide, the market places its greatest value. The comparative values can be worked out in a simplistic hand-held model inscribed in pen or pencil. They will be helpful as long as their purpose is kept in mind: to provoke the throwing off of new options for decision making.

When a demand model is used in this way, contingent strategy making can take place on an ongoing basis. An inventory of strategy options will always be available to deal with short-term changes in the as-if model of the market. With continuous strategy making, all planning can become contingency planning because it will be designed to be contingent on various changes as they occur or in anticipation of them.

If you elect to organize a consolidated planning and information system, use a separate copy of Planning Page 6 to construct an "As-if," "What-if?" interface of market values and strategy options for every market segment it will serve.

These three systems have been presented here in the rank order of their application to management problem solving. In terms of their actual integration with each other, their sequencing is exactly reversed. According to Exhibit 2-3, the planning and information system is the originator of fundamental strategy options. These, in turn, become inputs for the profit prediction and projection system. The bottom-line futures that issue from profit projection then become the raw data for the consultation and control system, which acts to make certain that funding, market knowledge, and technical capability can be employed with the greatest cost effectiveness to achieve planned objectives.

EXHIBIT 2-1

CONSULTATION AND CONTROL SYSTEM

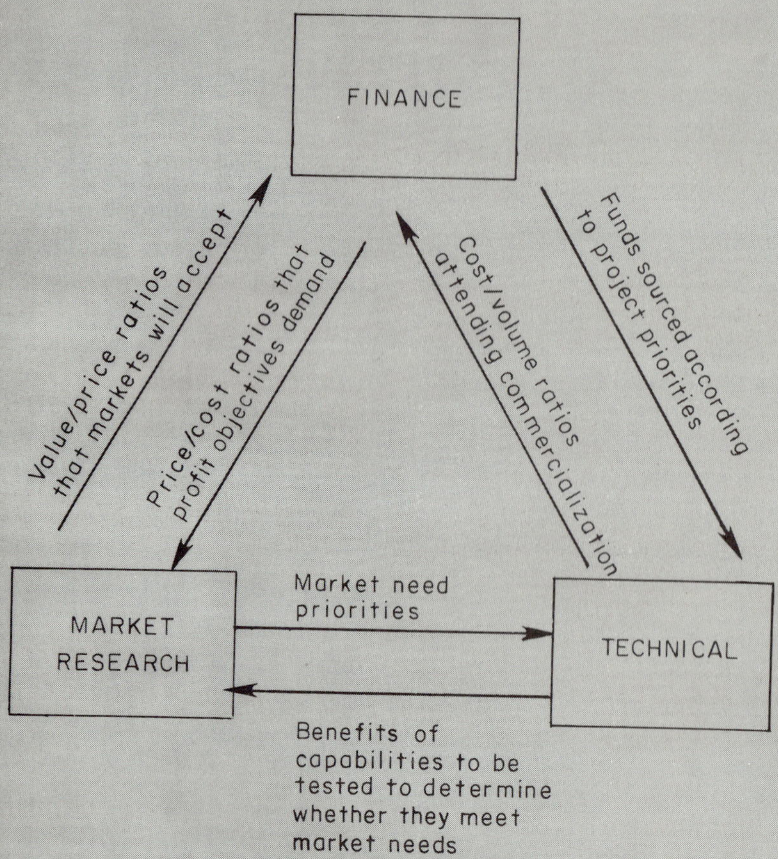

EXHIBIT 2-2

PROFIT PREDICTION AND PROJECTION SYSTEM

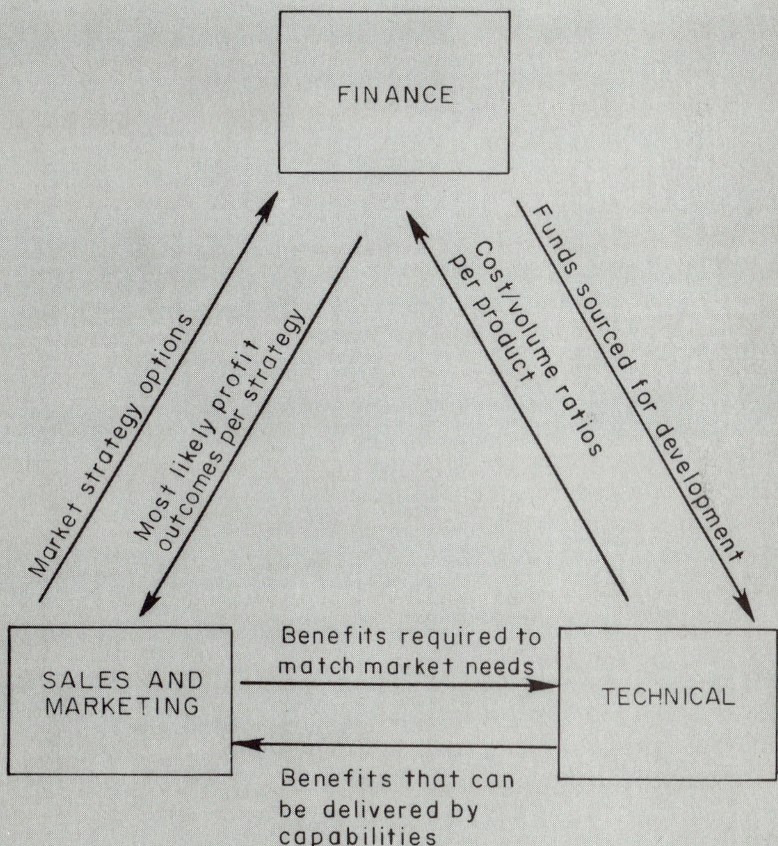

EXHIBIT 2-3

MANAGEMENT SYSTEMS OPERATIONAL SEQUENCING

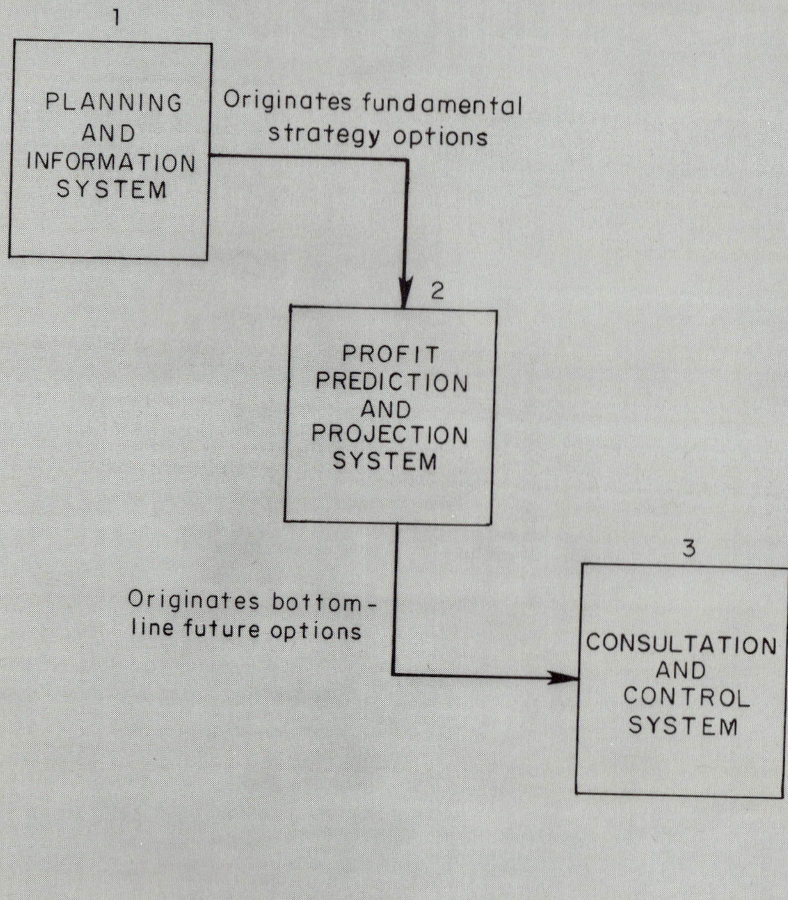

2-3 GROWTH MARKET TARGETING AND FAIR ASSUMPTIONS

All markets are gross. A gross market cannot be reached in a cost-effective manner. It is too heterogeneous. About 80 percent of every market contains light profit contributors. They buy seldom or sporadically. They use up or wear out slowly what they buy. They buy at the low end of the line. They disloyally sample competitive offerings. They are the fringe market.

The remaining 20 percent or so of every market is composed of heavy profit contributors. They are your core growth market. They support your business by returning the highest profitable sales volume. If you want to accelerate growth, you must target your heavy-profit-contributing market segment and concentrate the sale of your most profitable products to them.

Growth Market Targeting

To target your heavy profit contributors, isolate the customers who buy and use your most profitable products in the greatest quantities, use them up at the fastest rate of consumption, and repurchase them at book price in the greatest frequency. Heavy profit contributors rarely amount to more than 20 to 30 percent of a market's total potential and actual customers. Yet they can account for up to 80 percent of profitable sales volume. For a typical diversified marketer, it is not unusual to find that only 10 percent of all customers account for as much as 60 percent of all profitable sales volume.

The F. & M. Schaefer Brewing Company has been "willing to forsake all those people who drink a can of beer once every 2 weeks," preferring to concentrate on the 20 percent of all beer drinkers who drink 80 percent of all beer. To the members of this heavy-profit-contributor market segment who drink at least two cans of beer a day, Schaefer has said it is "the one beer to have when you're having more than one." In similar fashion, Coca-Cola markets primarily to the 10 percent of all soft-drink users who drink 60 percent of all Coca-Cola: "The restless people . . . who think of themselves as expending a lot of energy, who drink around the clock, at 11, at 2, at 4, drinking five or six Cokes throughout the day."

The criteria for heavy profit contribution vary with markets. The heavy contributor of profit to an aspirin manufacturer is most likely to be the young adult woman in an economically upscale family or the young-to-middle-aged man in a managerial job who throws off the profit from use of 2 dozen or more aspirin tablets a month. The heavy contributor of profit to a razor-blade manufacturer is the young-to-middle-aged white-collar man who prefers westerns and sports programs on television and who throws off the profit from use of three to five blades a week. The heavy contributor of profit to an airline is the business executive who throws off the profit from a minimum of twenty flights a year.

Heavy profit contributors in industry may be classified in similar fashion. The heavy contributor of profit to a refractory brick manufacturer is the steel-company furnace superintendent who throws off the profit from use of enough brick to melt a minimum of 1 million tons of steel every year.

Use a separate copy of Planning Page 7 to target each of your heavy-profit-contributing market segments. Identify it according to the Standard Industrial Classification (SIC) code and to the single most crucial benefit it needs from you. Define its size in terms of total gross sales volume this year and your share in terms of gross sales contribution and profit on sales. Then use a separate copy of Planning Page 8 to profile each market segment's heavy profit contributors. Define them according to their professional or personal position description, the minimum-usage criterion that qualifies them as heavy contributors, and a match-up of their needs with your product benefits on a product-by-product basis.

Life-styled market segmentation[1] is an approach to seizing the concept of a heavy-profit-contributing consumer market according to its most meaningful, repetitive patterns of attitudes and activities. Life-styling groups markets according to "systems" of interrelated attitudes and activities that create the need for products and services.

As an example, one important system of attitudes and activities can be called a woman homemaker's life-styled role as "family physician." In this role, which is spelled out as a scenario in Exhibit 2-4, the homemaker is thinking, feeling, and acting like a quasi-professional practitioner of nursing and medical functions. She is the home paramedic. Many of her concerns are the same as those of medical doctors and registered nurses in a hospital environment. But because she is in the home, the homemaker deprofessionalizes them. She meets her needs commercially, that is, through the purchase and use of health care products and information services. As a result of its commercial orientation, the family physician role can therefore be marketed to as a segment.

Exhibits 2-5 through 2-10 show six life-styled roles for the married woman homemaker that can form the need base for marketable segments: home economics management, personal care management, environmental management, travel and entertainment management, training and education management, and family business management. If you elect to market to the heavy profit contributors in any one or more of them, use a separate copy of Planning Page 9 to define each role in your own terms and work out the products and services you will market to it.

A heavy-profit-contributing market segment gained is not always a market maintained. Many events beyond your control can require you to retarget a profitable segment. For example, shortfalls of energy or raw

[1] A more detailed treatment of this subject can be found in Mack Hanan, *Life-Styled Marketing*, AMACOM, American Management Association, New York, 1972.

materials may wipe out your capability to supply a product line and thereby eliminate an entire group of customers as a market. Legislative proscription against ingredients such as hexachlorophene or propellants such as fluorocarbons may defy cost-effective reformulation or alter the basis of a market's preference. Even mere debate can be as injurious as fiat. Public controversy in the mid-1970s over whether fluorocarbon gases contained in spray cans could imperil the vital ozone layer over the earth significantly depressed the aerosol market even though the theory was unproved. During the first 6 months of the debate, shipments of spray cans dropped 26 percent from the level of the year before.

There are other ways in which your market segmentation can be affected. A segment may become disenfranchised by consumer boycott. Rising costs in the face of declining margins or low market shares may cause you to nip off even successful or highly promising products or services, no matter how strong their sales base continues to be. Price increases or undependable supply may drive customers into substitutes or condition them to doing without your product.

Even a historic market franchise provides uncertain continuity. In the automobile industry, the shift in preference to small cars forced manufacturers to alter their market strategy along with their production. The strategy of automobile manufacturers has always been based on customer loyalty. This has been especially true for General Motors, some of whose cars have enjoyed a brand repurchase rate of as much as 90 percent by the same owners. But with the trend to small cars, customer loyalty greatly decreased. Instead of relating to a specific brand, buyers of small cars began to base their decisions on the benefits of fuel economy, maintenance, and price.

Either in anticipation of events like these or as a result of them, you may need to retarget your market segments. You may decide to enter new markets. You may abandon some traditional markets just as General Electric and Westinghouse have left the market for heavy household appliances and Chrysler has pulled out of the luxury-car market. As a result, phrases like "full-line supplier," "multimarket manufacturer," and "broad-scale problem solver" may disappear from your charter. In other cases, a new characterization of your business such as "systems supplier" may become relevant as a growth capability.

EXHIBIT 2-4

"FAMILY PHYSICIAN" LIFE-STYLED SCENARIO

The mass, middle-majority married woman homemaker in her life-styled role as family physician is concerned essentially with the feeling, the appearance, and the substance of her family's health. In short, she wants family members to feel healthy, look healthy, and be healthy. Her primary role is health maintenance. In this aspect of her role, she thinks and acts very much like an insurance agent for her family. Her concerns are principally *preventive.* The second aspect of her role is acutely critical, generally overtaking her with little or no warning. This is the emergency *therapeutic* aspect of family health care. Insofar as possible, she places her reliance on routine maintenance to ward off emergencies. When they happen anyway in spite of her best efforts, she needs to feel prepared with appropriate products and information services as adequately as possible.

The attitude and activity pattern of family physician is extremely sober and serious. Health is never a laughing matter. The married woman homemaker is therefore best addressed when she is in this role as a rational, caring, protective, and businesslike person who carries a severe responsibility. Accordingly, products and information services designed to serve her must be exemplary in their dependability, reliability, and guaranteed performance.

EXHIBIT 2-5

LIFE-STYLED ROLES IN HOME ECONOMICS MANAGEMENT

1. **The married woman homemaker in her life-styled role as family dietician**

   The middle-majority homemaker, aged 19 to 49, in her roles as food selector and meal balancer, daily-menu planner, and culinary artisan and food stylist.

   Product and service system categories compatible with this role include foods, functional foods, and food analogs; meal-planning and menu-planning consultation services; recipe services; food-styling consultation and education services; fast-food franchise services; computerized food ordering and delivery services; and televised or franchised cooking schools.

2. **The married woman homemaker in her life-styled role as food systems engineer**

   The middle-majority homemaker, aged 19 to 49, in her role as skilled operator of food storage, cooking, serving, and disposal systems; meal-planning and menu-rationalizing systems; and utensil-cleaning, maintenance, and storage systems.

   Product and service system categories compatible with this role include household appliance systems, appliance layout consultation services, appliance operation consultation services, appliance maintenance and repair services, service contract consultation service or books, disposable-utensil product lines, detergents and ultrasonic cleaning systems, and appliance rental services.

EXHIBIT 2-6

LIFE-STYLED ROLES IN PERSONAL CARE MANAGEMENT

1. **The married woman homemaker in her life-styled role as personal health care manager**

   The middle-majority homemaker, aged 19 to 59, in her roles as family physician and nurse and family physical health and mental health educator.

   Product and service system categories compatible with this role include internally and externally applied drugs, health foods, and functional foods; computerized health care and consultation services: self-diagnostic kits; clinics and care centers; disposable products; health education services and media; and feminine-hygiene products and services.

2. **The married woman homemaker in her life-styled role as personal beauty and grooming care manager**

   The middle-majority homemaker, aged 19 to 59, in her roles as socially attractive woman in public situations and seductively attractive wife or lover in private situations.

   Product and service system categories compatible with this role include internal beauty care products such as beauty foods and beauty drugs, including psychedelic drugs; external beauty care products such as hair, face, and body cosmetics; fashionable apparel and accessories; and beauty care services such as beauty consultation and product prescription services, computerized complexion analysis, self-styling systems of beauty care, and shops, salons, or shopping services.

EXHIBIT 2-7

LIFE-STYLED ROLES IN ENVIRONMENTAL MANAGEMENT

1. **The married woman homemaker in her life-styled role as internal environment creator and manager**

   The middle-majority homemaker, aged 19 to 59, in her roles as interior decorator and mood stylist for the home, cottage craftsman, equity-building collector, communications systems manager, home repairman and service contract negotiator with external repair and manufacturing services, and family maid and sanitary engineer.

   Product and service system categories compatible with this role include interior decoration consultation services and media, home repair kits and manuals, home furnishings for sale or rent, in-home communications systems, home repair contractual and insurance services, modular home study centers and work carrels, rental maid services, bathroom equipment and fixtures, saunas, household appliance and furnishings insurance services, and service contract consultation services.

2. **The married woman homemaker in her life-styled role as external environment creator and manager**

   The middle-majority homemaker, aged 19 to 59, in her roles as architect and home builder, gardener and landscaper, outdoor living equipment and systems planner, general property value manager, and service contract negotiator with external repair and manufacturing services.

   Product and service system categories compatible with this role include home rental or purchasing consultation services; home improvement products and services; home repair kits and manuals, property value maintenance instruction and information services; gardening tools, seeds, and planning services; synthetic lawns and other home decoration products and services; landscape rental services; disposable landscaping; landscape insurance; children's yard and porch structures and exercise equipment; pools and solaria; and service contract consultation.

EXHIBIT 2-8

LIFE-STYLED ROLES IN TRAVEL AND ENTERTAINMENT MANAGEMENT

1. **The married woman homemaker in her life-styled role as family travel agent**

   The middle-majority homemaker, aged 19 to 59, in her roles as vacation selector and planner.

   Product and service system categories compatible with this role include vacation-styling services; vacation packs of portable foods, drugs, and cosmetics: disposable vacation apparel and accessories; and computerized vacation-planning services.

2. **The married woman homemaker in her life-styled role as family entertainment director.**

   The middle-majority homemaker, aged 19 to 49, in her roles as amusement selector and censor, leisure-time planner, toy and game buyer, arts and crafts hobbyist and buyer, and family athletic director and coach.

   Product and service system categories compatible with this role include leisure-time planning services; toy, game, and craft products; hobbyist products; athletic equipment and instruction services; athletics-oriented cosmetics and quick-energy foods; first-aid equipment and preventive or remedial products such as suntan lotions and sprays or pills, aerosol bandages, and hot and cold packs; picnic and camping equipment; outdoor patio and backyard living equipment; sporting clubs and groups; country clubs; boats; and skis or skimobile manufacturing and rental services.

EXHIBIT 2-9

LIFE-STYLED ROLES IN TRAINING AND EDUCATION MANAGEMENT

1. **The married woman homemaker in her life-styled role as baby mother and trainer**

   The middle-majority homemaker, aged 19 to 39, in her roles as baby entertainer and teacher.

   Product and service system categories compatible with this role include baby care instruction and education books, films, classes, and other consultation services; toys and games; baby accessories, apparel, and disposables; and reward-type foods.

2. **The married woman homemaker in her life-styled role as child trainer and educator**

   The middle-majority homemaker, aged 19 to 49, in her roles as child entertainer and teacher.

   Product and service system categories compatible with this role include child care instruction and education books, films, classes, and other consultation services; children's toys, games, and crafts; children's preschool educational services and tools; children's accessories, apparel, and equipment for school; disposable training and education aids; child health insurance; and children's college enrollment insurance.

3. **The married woman homemaker in her life-styled role as pet trainer and educator**

   The middle-majority homemaker, aged 19 to 49, in her roles as animal and bird purchaser, feeder, teacher, entertainer, and health manager.

   Product and service system categories compatible with this role include franchised kennels and aviaries; pet foods; pet accessories, disposable apparel, and toys; pet care instruction services; pet health insurance; and pet care and maintenance services.

EXHIBIT 2-10

LIFE-STYLED ROLES IN FAMILY BUSINESS MANAGEMENT

1. **The married woman homemaker in her life-styled role as family money manager.**

   The middle-majority homemaker, aged 19 to 59, in her roles as family treasurer and credit manager, family accountant and budgeter, and family estate executor.

   Product and service system categories compatible with this role include household budget-planning educational services and computerized budget-keeping services, investment advisory services, and food budget-planning guides.

2. **The married woman homemaker in her life-styled role as family purchasing agent**

   The middle-majority homemaker, aged 19 to 49, in her roles as comparison shopper, buyer, and order taker within the family.

   Product and service system categories compatible with this role include shopping consultation services; buyer education classes, books, films, and television programs; product comparison services; labeling and packaging guides for smart shopping; and gift suggestion and purchasing services.

Fair-Assumption Making

Growth market targeting, whether by life styling or by other forms of segmentation, is designed to provide the external fact base for accelerated profit making. Once we identify a target market's propensity to buy in a volume and at a price that can provide a heavy profit contribution, we tend to think that we have seized the nature of the market. But we have, at best, only gained an understanding of its past. Since growth is future-oriented, we must find a way to get a fix on what a market will do in the near term from which its incremental profit contribution will come.

In the interval between the point at which our knowledge of a market's past propensities leaves off and the near-term future begins, many factors can impinge on the nature of our target. Some of these factors will be benign: they will help reinforce our accelerated growth strategies. Other factors will constrain them. At the time when we plan to target on a heavy-profit-contributor segment, it may look good to us. But there is no way to guarantee that it will stay that way. We can assume that it will, but our plans will be only as good as our assumptions.

Growth planning is an assumptive process. The belief that a business can be grown at an accelerated rate is an assumption. Objectives that seek to quantify growth are assumptions. Although they may be based on hard or semihard numbers, growth objectives themselves are always soft. Strategies created to achieve objectives are also assumptions. They represent a mix of the best assumptions about the most cost-effective way to achieve growth objectives.

Experience shows that few of us, even professional planners, make good assumptions. In 1970 most planners foresaw the upcoming decade opportunistically. They predicted vigorous economic growth that would increase demand for raw materials. But they did not foresee worldwide shortages in metals, timber products, food, and fuel. Nor did they foresee the cartelization of oil-producing countries that could mandate a fourfold increase in the price of crude petroleum. The planners foresaw a continuing inflationary trend. But they did not predict a rate of price increase of 12 percent in the United States and far higher elsewhere. The planners foresaw increasing government intervention in assuring basic product quality and advertising probity, occupational safety and health, and environmental protection. But they did not predict the scale of regulation or the costs that it would impose for compliance. Finally, the planners foresaw the rising demand for investment money. But they underestimated the sum total of equity and debt financing that would be created by combined needs for expansion, modernization, and compliance, and they failed to anticipate the increased interest rates and the financial-market breakdown that deprived businesses of their traditional sources of capital.

Assumptions are the heart and soul of growth planning. The central talent they require is the ability to foresee the future impact of a present decision. This is not an ability to foretell the future. It is a predictive "sense of outcome" in answer to the question *"If we were to do this, what would be most likely to happen?"*

Predictive skill is unevenly distributed. There are good sensers of outcome and poor sensers. The mythology of growth planning has itself been based on an assumption. The crux of skillful prediction has been simplistically said to center on "getting the facts." But this is only half the equation and probably the lesser half. The true crux of being able to sense outcomes, as we see it, is focused not on getting the facts but on interpreting them. This is an entirely different aptitude. Fact getting is a reporter's function. Interpretation is a manager's function.

Three Major Sources of Error

Interpretation as we define it is the prior assessment of impact. In growth planning, a fact does not exist if it is not assessed as having impact on the plan. Even though it is a real-world event, it will not have occurred if the growth planner does not perceive that it will have a benign or constraining effect on the plan's objectives.

We therefore deal only with facts that tend to have an impact. This is our first level of assumption. That is, it is our first opportunity to be wrong. If we inadvisably screen out a fact at this level from an assessment of its impact, we will never know what hit us when the error comes home to roost. Impacts of this kind can destroy growth plans because we are totally unprepared for them. In defense, we claim that the damage occurred out of a clear blue sky. We learn, usually later rather than earlier, that in growth planning there are no clear blue skies.

Overlooking a fact that is likely to have an impact is what we call a "threshold type of assumption." When we make it, we are at the gateway to the assessment process of sensing an outcome. Once past the gateway, we have our second opportunity to be wrong. This can come from our inability to make a correct interpretation of what a fact means to us. At this point, we are past the threshold. We have agreed that a fact has meaning for us. Now we must interpret that meaning. Otherwise, we will not be able to apply the fact.

It takes most of us a while to learn that facts themselves are meaningless, and it almost always comes as a surprise when we do. Facts are literally without meaning until we interpret them. It is our interpretation that gives them life. We can carry this reasoning further and say that facts themselves are useless without interpretation. The significant question we must ask is not "What does it say?" but "What does it mean?" Our answer is another assumption: an allegation that something will happen. We think of impacts as alleged impacts.

Times of swift and significant change lessen the degree of confidence we can assign to making interpretations that are based on projections from current facts. What happened yesterday is less and less a reliable guide to what may happen tomorrow. The basis of yesterday's facts is susceptible to alterations that invalidate using them as points of departure for trends and tendencies. Inflation destroys cost bases. Business cycle swings and compliance legislation destroy earnings bases. Energy and materials shortfalls destroy sales bases. Technological change may destroy a competitive base. If we try to plot a straight-line movement of a meaning from the past, we can have our third opportunity to make an incorrect assumption. Not only may there be no straight line; there may not even be a wavy one.

Facts we overlook because we fail to assign meaning to them, facts whose meaning we misinterpret, and facts we try to project after the basis for projection has been demolished are the three major sources of error in the assumption-making process. Avoiding these three harpies is the most crucial imperative of growth planning. In planning for accelerated growth, we learn that it is not the act of amassing and assessing a fact base that determines success. This is prelude. The assumptive base is the jumping-off place to unusual achievement. Growth, the ultimate assumption, is founded on assumptions. This is the genesis of entrepreneurial risk and the justification of the intensity and rarity of its rewards.

Ten Areas for Assumption Making

In extending today's market targeting into the future, there are ten variable factors about which assumptions may have to be made. They represent areas of potential change. Not all markets require making assumptions in all ten areas. That can be stated as a fact. But the determination of just which change areas must be assumed, and how, is the key assumption in growth planning.

We believe that the ten assumptive areas can best be identified as follows:

1. Economic changes
2. Legislative changes
3. Market changes
4. Technological changes
5. Competitive changes
6. Management changes
7. Labor force changes

8. Supply changes
9. Consumerist changes
10. Value changes

Assumptions in any of these areas are attempts to forecast a future outcome. It is easy to maneuver them so that the future you prefer is the one that you assume. The comfort factor in operating in this way vastly exceeds the accuracy factor. As a result, many assumptions are made at the 50 percent level of probability or lower. By our definition, this means that they are guesses, not assumptions. We believe that an assumption has planning validity only if it has been forced into the narrow confines of a 90 percent probability. We call this approach to forecasting "90 percent probability assumption making." We call the assumptions that come out of this process "fair assumptions"—fair to the markets they concern. By forcing assumption making to the 90 percent probability level, you confirm to yourself that you have enough confidence in the probability of a market change or market stability to bet on it by using it as the base for your growth objectives and your growth strategy mix.

Use Planning Pages 10 through 19 to make fair assumptions about each of the ten areas of potential change that can affect your target market. Spell out every assumption with exactitude. Then use Planning Pages 10a through 19a to assess the alleged impact of every change on your market. Some of your assumptions about impacts will be benign. They will support your growth thrust. Other assumptions will constrain it. The benign impacts you assume are the signal events on which your growth depends. They are your "facts." Use Planning Page 20 to analyze the assumptions on which your growth depends and record them as the basis for setting your growth objectives. On at least a quarterly basis thereafter, monitor your assumptions to make sure that allegedly benign assumptions remain benign. If one or more of them turns sour and begins to become a constraint or even seriously threatens to do so, you must consider resetting your objectives and creating a revised strategy mix.

2-4 GROWTH SOURCE CATEGORIZATION AND GROWTH OBJECTIVE SETTING

Four business or product categories are sources of accelerated growth. Three of these categories offer brand-building opportunities: new products, existing brands, and premature commodities. The fourth category consists of rebrandable-commodity businesses. These categories are shown in their traditional positions on the life-cycle curve in Exhibit 2-11.

EXHIBIT 2-11

THE FOUR CATEGORIES FOR ACCELERATED GROWTH

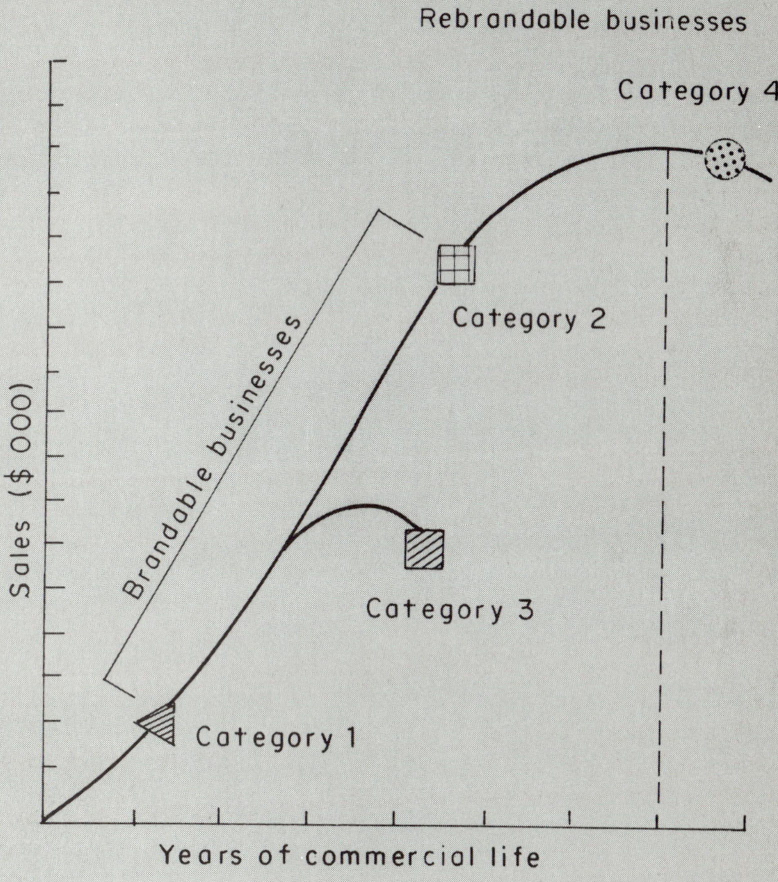

Growth Source Categorization

Of the four business or product categories, the most difficult to grow at an accelerated rate are Categories 1 and 3: new products and premature commodities. New products are difficult to grow because they possess the inherent inertia of a start-up business. Like all bodies at rest, they tend to remain at rest. Only the highly skilled application of market penetration strategies can move them. Since new products already represent a sizable investment in sunk costs, the growth thrust that is put behind them must be exceedingly cost-effective as well as skillful. Premature commodities can be doubly difficult because they must first be repositioned very much like new products before their growth can be accelerated.

Accelerating the growth of existing brands can often be the easiest strategy to implement. Category 2 products have one advantage going for them that is shared only with some new products: they are already growing at a speeded rate. The major difficulty they present is predictive. It is usually problematic to estimate accurately the amount of new profit that can be added to their current accelerated growth so that incremental growth investments can be made cost-effectively. Mature commodities present greater difficulty than brands because they rarely possess the entrepreneurial management, marketcentered organization or operating style, or budgetary availability necessary to rebrand them. Their markets are frequently more willing to accept their rebranding than their managers are able to rebrand them.

The essential reason why Categories 2 and 4 offer a lower degree of difficulty to growth acceleration than Categories 1 and 3 is that brands and mature commodities are generally clean-cut. They are readily identifiable for what they are. Few arguments are provoked over their status. Contrariwise, a new product can be anything that anyone wants it to be until it proves or disproves itself. It can be nothing, or it can be everything up to and including its sponsor's belief that it is the corporate savior. This makes it an either-or proposition. A premature commodity's difficulty comes because it is a neither-nor proposition. It is neither success nor failure but a gray in-between.

Use Planning Page 21 to categorize your potential growth sources in the three brand-building categories and the one rebranding category. Relate each growth source to its heavy-profit-contributor market. Then use Planning Pages 22 and 23 to quantify their contributions.

Growth Objective Setting

We prefer to work with eight quantified objectives for incremental growth thrusts. Because growth is incremental—that is, it makes a contribution over and above budgeted profit goals—we think of growth objectives as "microobjectives." This allows us to set them apart from overall corporate or departmental "macroobjectives" so that we can measure their additive impact. The eight objectives we recommend are spelled out on Planning Page 22, where they are subdivided into five *financial objectives* and three *sales objectives:*

1. Return on investment.
2. Net profit after taxes, with specific emphasis on the incremental profit gain that is yielded by stepping up growth. This increment represents the true value added by subsidizing growth.
3. Cash flow.
4. Annual earnings growth contribution.
5. Margin over average return on total corporate assets.
6. Unit sales volume.
7. Dollar sales volume.
8. Market share.

Of the eight objectives we set for a business that is under an accelerated growth thrust, the single most important objective is the return we can expect on the specific investment in assets allocated to obtain the business's growth. This is our ultimate test of the worthwhileness of growth. We also want to know aftertax net profit (NPAT). We regard NPAT as our key index of capital generation because aftertax profit is what we can take to the bank. Further, we want to know the ability of every growth thrust to contribute cash flow over the course of its life cycle.

As inflation continues to make comparative growth achievements less and less meaningful, we like to use a base year whose dollar value of earnings remains a constant standard for comparison. Then, for our fifth financial objective, we set down the average rate of return that the total corporation makes on assets and try to exceed it by the greatest possible margin. This becomes our criterion for the "quality" of every growth thrust. The greater the margin by which a growth thrust exceeds the return-on-total-corporate-assets bogey, the higher its quality.

To pin down the source of support for our financial objectives, we also forecast the three sales objectives that are predictors of revenue: unit and dollar sales volume and percentage share of market.

It is useful for us to view growth not only in absolute terms but also comparatively in the form of *critical ratios.* We use four ratios. The first is return on investment (ROI), the ratio of profit to investment. We supplement ROI with three other critical ratios: gross profit on sales, which yields gross margin; net profit on sales; and capital turnover, which compares the sales dollars generated by every dollar of investment. When we multiply net profit on sales by capital turnover, we have another way of assessing ROI.

The Three Categories for Objectives

You will notice on Planning Pages 22 and 23 that we like to apply sensitivity analysis to our objectives for quantifying and qualifying growth. We sensitize growth by working with three categories for every objective: a "most likely" objective, a "best case" objective, and a "worst case" objective.

Most likely objectives are central. These are the achievements that we assume can be brought home with a 90 percent level of probability. In this regard, they correlate with our 90 percent probability assumptions. The most likely assumptions become the foundation for the most likely objectives.

For an objective to deserve an assessment of 90 percent probability of achievement, it must be unhaloed by what you believe that the business *should do* or what you might hope that the business under thrust *could do*. It commits you to what the business *is most likely to do*.

A 90 percent probability objective is essential to all growth planning. It takes on an even greater importance for your first-year objectives. These are the objectives that must tell you if and when a new business can reach break-even and be able to stand on its own feet. New business or old, your first-year objectives are the base line from which all successive annual objectives will be projected. If they are wrong, all subsequent objectives will perpetuate the error and perhaps even magnify it.

We surround the most likely objectives with two other categories. One is a best-case objective. This is a strawman objective, a number that we expect to achieve only at a 50 percent level of probability. It sets the high-water mark of achievement that we may be able to reach if the most critical factors in our plan work out to perfection or if unusual good luck comes to us. Best-case objectives are possible but not probable. Nonetheless, they are useful guides to defining how high up can be so that we can perceive our maximum upside reward. They also help put the most likely objectives in perspective.

The third category of objectives consists of the worst-case objectives, which reflect our maximum downside risk. We treat them as the threshold objectives for going ahead. If the threshold is below the average return on total corporate assets, we cannot commit our business to grow. For this reason, we charge ourselves with the responsibility for making our worst-case estimate come as close as possible to 100 percent probability. We dare not be surprised after crossing a threshold to find that we do not have a growth business. Since our worst-case objectives have not yet happened at the time when we project them (they may never happen; we hope they do not), we cannot achieve the 100 percent probability that only a fact can have. We therefore deal with these objectives as quasifacts and press hard on ourselves so that we are able to believe in them at a 99.9 percent level of probability.

Democratizing Growth Objectives

The formation of growth objectives, once the province of a select few managers, is becoming democratized. Different people, and often more of them, are involved in formulating growth. Still others are participating in reviewing and revising growth objectives.

Growth groups, objective formulation councils, goal formation committees, and growth review committees are increasingly popular devices. Participants can be drawn from several organization functions: sales and marketing, finance, R&D, and product development.

On Planning Page 24, set up a growth-objectives formation team (F team). Then on Planning Page 25, organize a growth-objectives review and revision team (R&R team) to act as a gadfly and counterbalance to the formation team. The formation team will have the exclusive right to propose growth objectives. The review and revision team will have the right of review and the right to recommend revisions to the formation team on new copies of Planning Page 23. Appoint yourself chairman and sole joint member of both teams, and convene them at least monthly.

PLANNING PAGES
1–25

CONCENTRATED BUSINESS POSITIONING STATEMENTS

Business: ______________________________

Heavy-profit-contributor market: SIC # ______ Industry classification ______________________

or consumer life-style ______________________

1. Businesss Positioning

After branding (rebranding), this business will be positioned as "the only business that (identify the single most crucial benefit to be conferred on heavy-profit-contributor market)

____"

2. Product positionings

Product ______: "This product will be the only product that (single most crucial benefit)

____"

Product ______: "This product will be the only product that (single most crucial benefit)

____"

Product ______: "This product will be the only product that (single most crucial benefit)

____"

CONCENTRATED BUSINESS POSITIONING STATEMENTS

Business: ______________________________

Heavy-profit-contributor market: SIC # ______ Industry classification ______________

or consumer life-style ______________

1. Businesss Positioning

After branding (rebranding), this business will be positioned as "the only business that (identify the single most crucial benefit to be conferred on heavy-profit-contributor market)

______________________________"

2. Product positionings

Product ______: "This product will be the only product that (single most crucial benefit)

______________________________"

Product ______: "This product will be the only product that (single most crucial benefit)

______________________________"

Product ______: "This product will be the only product that (single most crucial benefit)

______________________________"

CONCENTRATED BUSINESS POSITIONING STATEMENTS

Business: ______________________________

Heavy-profit-contributor market: SIC # ______ Industry classification ______________________

or consumer life-style ______________________

1. Businesss Positioning

After branding (rebranding), this business will be positioned as "the only business that (identify the single most crucial benefit to be conferred on heavy-profit-contributor market)

____"

2. Product positionings

Product ______: "This product will be the only product that (single most crucial benefit)

____"

Product ______: "This product will be the only product that (single most crucial benefit)

____"

Product ______: "This product will be the only product that (single most crucial benefit)

____"

PROFIT-DOMINANCE OBJECTIVES

Business: ______________________________

First year (19__) most likely objectives

1. Return on growth thrust investment
   (Micro %) --%

2. Net profit after taxes
   ($000) $__,___

3. Cash flow
   ($000) $__,___

PROFIT-DOMINANCE OBJECTIVES

Business: ______________________________

First year (19__) most likely objectives

1. Return on growth thrust investment
   (Micro %) --%

2. Net profit after taxes
   ($000) $--,---

3. Cash flow
   ($000) $--,---

PROFIT-DOMINANCE OBJECTIVES

Business: ______________________________

First year (19__) most likely objectives

1. Return on growth thrust investment (Micro %) __%

2. Net profit after taxes ($000) $__,___

3. Cash flow ($000) $__,___

FUNCTIONAL CONCENTRATION PLAN

Business: ______________________________

Functions	Staff allocations	Budget allocations ($000)
1. Information resourcing and market research	#___	$__,___
2. Sales	#___	$__,___
3. Finance	#___	$__,___
4. Product development and R&D	#___	$__,___
5.	#___	$__,___
6.	#___	$__,___

FUNCTIONAL CONCENTRATION PLAN

Business: ______________________________

Functions	Staff allocations	Budget allocations ($000)
1. Information resourcing and market research	#___	$__,___
2. Sales	#___	$__,___
3. Finance	#___	$__,___
4. Product development and R&D	#___	$__,___
5.	#___	$__,___
6.	#___	$__,___

FUNCTIONAL CONCENTRATION PLAN

Business: ______________________________

Functions	Staff allocations	Budget allocations ($000)
1. Information resourcing and market research	#___	$__,___
2. Sales	#___	$__,___
3. Finance	#___	$__,___
4. Product development and R&D	#___	$__,___
5.	#___	$__,___
6.	#___	$__,___

CONSULTATION AND CONTROL SYSTEM

To serve SIC #______ Industry classification ____________
or consumer life-style ____________

Priority rank order of most profitable problems to be solved	Most cost-effective short-term solution strategy
1. ____________	1. ____________
2. ____________	2. ____________
3. ____________	3. ____________
4. ____________	4. ____________
5. ____________	5. ____________

CONSULTATION AND CONTROL SYSTEM

To serve SIC #______ Industry classification ____________
or consumer life-style ____________

Priority rank order of most profitable problems to be solved	Most cost-effective short-term solution strategy
1. ____________	1. ____________ ____________
2. ____________	2. ____________ ____________
3. ____________	3. ____________ ____________
4. ____________	4. ____________ ____________
5. ____________	5. ____________ ____________

CONSULTATION AND CONTROL SYSTEM

To serve SIC #______ Industry classification ______________
or consumer life-style ______________

Priority rank order of most profitable problems to be solved	Most cost-effective short-term solution strategy
1. ______________	1. ______________
2. ______________	2. ______________
3. ______________	3. ______________
4. ______________	4. ______________
5. ______________	5. ______________

PROFIT PREDICTION AND PROJECTION SYSTEM

To serve SIC # ______ Industry classification ____________________

or consumer life-style ____________________

	"What-if?" solution strategy	Strategy investment base	Most likely profit outcomes ($000) Year 1 (19__)	Year 2 (19__)	Year 3 (19__)
1.	____________	$___,___,___	$___,___	$___,___	$___,___
2.	____________	___,___,___	___,___	___,___	___,___
3.	____________	___,___,___	___,___	___,___	___,___
4.	____________	___,___,___	___,___	___,___	___,___
5.	____________	___,___,___	___,___	___,___	___,___

PROFIT PREDICTION AND PROJECTION SYSTEM

To serve SIC # ______ Industry classification ______________________

or consumer life-style ______________________

	"What-if?" solution strategy	Strategy investment base	Most likely profit outcomes ($000) Year 1 (19__)	Year 2 (19__)	Year 3 (19__)
1.	______________	$___,___,___	$___,___	$___,___	$___,___
2.	______________	___,___,___	___,___	___,___	___,___
3.	______________	___,___,___	___,___	___,___	___,___
4.	______________	___,___,___	___,___	___,___	___,___
5.	______________	___,___,___	___,___	___,___	___,___

PROFIT PREDICTION AND PROJECTION SYSTEM

To serve SIC # ______ Industry classification ______________________

or consumer life-style ______________________

"What-if?" solution strategy	Strategy investment base	Most likely profit outcomes ($000)		
		Year 1 (19__)	Year 2 (19__)	Year 3 (19__)
1. ________________	$___,___,___	$___,___	$___,___	$___,___
2. ________________	___,___,___	___,___	___,___	___,___
3. ________________	___,___,___	___,___	___,___	___,___
4. ________________	___,___,___	___,___	___,___	___,___
5. ________________	___,___,___	___,___	___,___	___,___

HEAVY-PROFIT-CONTRIBUTOR MARKET SEGMENT TARGETER

SIC #__________ Industry classification ____________________

or consumer life-style ____________________

This market is composed of needers of (single most crucial benefit) ______________________________

____

Total industry sales volume this year #000	Total industry sales volume this year $000	Gross sales contribution $000	Profit on sales $000
#---,---	$---,---	$---,---	$---,---

PLANNING AND INFORMATION SYSTEM

To serve SIC #______ Industry classification __________

or consumer life-style __________

"As-if" market values	"What-if?" strategy options
1. __________	1. __________
2. __________	2. __________
3. __________	3. __________
4. __________	4. __________
5. __________	5. __________

PLANNING AND INFORMATION SYSTEM

To serve SIC #______ Industry classification ______________

or consumer life-style ______________

"As-if" market values	"What-if?" strategy options
1. ______________	1. ______________
	______________
	______________
2. ______________	2. ______________
	______________
	______________
3. ______________	3. ______________
	______________
	______________
4. ______________	4. ______________
	______________
	______________
5. ______________	5. ______________
	______________
	______________

PLANNING AND INFORMATION SYSTEM

To serve SIC #______ Industry classification __________

or consumer life-style __________

"As-if" market values	"What-if?" strategy options
1. __________	1. __________
2. __________	2. __________
3. __________	3. __________
4. __________	4. __________
5. __________	5. __________

HEAVY-PROFIT-CONTRIBUTOR
MARKET SEGMENT TARGETER

SIC #________ Industry classification ________________

or consumer life-style ________________

This market is composed of needers of (single most crucial benefit) ________________________

____

Total industry sales volume this year		Gross sales contribution	Profit on sales
#000	$000	$000	$000
#---,---	$---,---	$---,---	$---,---

HEAVY-PROFIT-CONTRIBUTOR MARKET SEGMENT TARGETER

SIC #__________ Industry classification __________________

or consumer life-style __________________

This market is composed of needers of (single most crucial benefit) __________________________

____

Total industry sales volume this year #000	$000	Gross sales contribution $000	Profit on sales $000
#---,---	$---,---	$---,---	$---,---

HEAVY-PROFIT-CONTRIBUTOR PROFILER

SIC # ____________ Industry classification ____________________

or consumer life-style ____________________

Professional or personal position description	Minimum-usage criterion Volume/time frame used	Needs/product and service match-up

Planning Page 8

HEAVY-PROFIT-CONTRIBUTOR PROFILER

SIC # __________ Industry classification __________________

or consumer life-style __________________

Professional or personal position description	Minimum-usage criterion Volume/time frame used	Needs/product and service match-up

HEAVY-PROFIT-CONTRIBUTOR PROFILER

SIC # ____________ Industry classification ____________________

or consumer life-style ____________________

Professional or personal position description	Minimum-usage criterion Volume/time frame used	Needs/product and service match-up

HEAVY-PROFIT-CONTRIBUTOR LIFE-STYLE ROLE

IN ______________________________

1. Title of role: ______________________________

2. Description of role player's attitude and activity pattern:

____

____

____

____

____

3. Product and service categories compatible with this role:

3.1. ______________________________

3.2. ______________________________

3.3. ______________________________

3.4. ______________________________

3.5. ______________________________

HEAVY-PROFIT-CONTRIBUTOR LIFE-STYLE ROLE

IN ______________________________

1. Title of role: ______________________________

2. Description of role player's attitude and activity pattern:

____

____

____

____

____

3. Product and service categories compatible with this role:

3.1. ______________________________

3.2. ______________________________

3.3. ______________________________

3.4. ______________________________

3.5. ______________________________

HEAVY-PROFIT-CONTRIBUTOR LIFE-STYLE ROLE

IN ______________________________

1. Title of role: ______________________________

2. Description of role player's attitude and activity pattern:

____

____

____

____

____

3. Product and service categories compatible with this role:

3.1. ______________________________

3.2. ______________________________

3.3. ______________________________

3.4. ______________________________

3.5. ______________________________

HEAVY-PROFIT-CONTRIBUTOR LIFE-STYLE ROLE

IN ______________________________

1. Title of role: ______________________________

2. Description of role player's attitude and activity pattern:

____

____

____

____

____

3. Product and service categories compatible with this role:

   3.1. ______________________________

   3.2. ______________________________

   3.3. ______________________________

   3.4. ______________________________

   3.5. ______________________________

ECONOMIC CHANGE ASSUMPTION

1. Assumed GNP growth rate --%

2. Assumed inflation rate --%

ECONOMIC CHANGE IMPACT ASSESSMENT

Target market SIC #________ Industry classification ________________

or consumer life-style ________________

I assess at the 90 percent level of confidence that the impact on my target market of the economic changes I have assumed on Planning Page 10 will be:

Nature of impact

____

____

____

____

____

Growth strategies that will be affected and how

1. ______________________________
2. ______________________________
3. ______________________________
4. ______________________________
5. ______________________________

LEGISLATIVE CHANGE ASSUMPTION

LEGISLATIVE CHANGE IMPACT ASSESSMENT

Target market SIC #________ Industry classification ________________

or consumer life-style ________________

I assess at the 90 percent level of confidence that the impact on my target market of the legislative changes I have assumed on Planning Page 11 will be:

Nature of impact

____

____

____

____

____

Growth strategies that will be affected and how

1. ______________________________________
2. ______________________________________
3. ______________________________________
4. ______________________________________
5. ______________________________________

MARKET CHANGE ASSUMPTION

MARKET CHANGE IMPACT ASSESSMENT

Target market SIC #__________ Industry classification ____________________

or consumer life-style ____________________

I assess at the 90 percent level of confidence that the impact on my target market of the market changes I have assumed on Planning Page 12 will be:

Nature of impact

____

____

____

____

____

Growth strategies that will be affected and how

1. ______________________________________
2. ______________________________________
3. ______________________________________
4. ______________________________________
5. ______________________________________

TECHNOLOGICAL CHANGE ASSUMPTION

TECHNOLOGICAL CHANGE IMPACT ASSESSMENT

Target market SIC #__________ Industry classification ____________________

or consumer life-style ____________________

I assess at the 90 percent level of confidence that the impact on my target market of the technological changes I have assumed on Planning Page 13 will be:

Nature of impact

____

____

____

____

____

Growth strategies that will be affected and how

1. ______________________________________
2. ______________________________________
3. ______________________________________
4. ______________________________________
5. ______________________________________

COMPETITIVE CHANGE ASSUMPTION

COMPETITIVE CHANGE IMPACT ASSESSMENT

Target market SIC #__________ Industry classification ____________________

or consumer life-style ____________________

I assess at the 90 percent level of confidence that the impact on my target market of the competitive changes I have assumed on Planning Page 14 will be:

Nature of impact

____

____

____

____

____

Growth strategies that will be affected and how

1. ______________________________
2. ______________________________
3. ______________________________
4. ______________________________
5. ______________________________

MANAGEMENT CHANGE ASSUMPTION

MANAGEMENT CHANGE IMPACT ASSESSMENT

Target market SIC #__________ Industry classification ____________________

or consumer life-style ____________________

I assess at the 90 percent level of confidence that the impact on my target market of the management changes I have assumed on Planning Page 15 will be:

Nature of impact

____

____

____

____

____

Growth strategies that will be affected and how

1. ____
2. ____
3. ____
4. ____
5. ____

LABOR FORCE CHANGE ASSUMPTION

LABOR FORCE CHANGE IMPACT ASSESSMENT

Target market SIC #________ Industry classification ______________

or consumer life-style ______________

I assess at the 90 percent level of confidence that the impact on my target market of the labor force changes I have assumed on Planning Page 16 will be:

Nature of impact

____

____

____

____

____

Growth strategies that will be affected and how

1. ______________________________
2. ______________________________
3. ______________________________
4. ______________________________
5. ______________________________

SUPPLY CHANGE ASSUMPTION

SUPPLY CHANGE IMPACT ASSESSMENT

Target market SIC #__________ Industry classification ____________________

or consumer life-style ____________________

I assess at the 90 percent level of confidence that the impact on my target market of the supply changes I have assumed on Planning Page 17 will be:

Nature of impact

____

____

____

____

____

Growth strategies that will be affected and how

1. ____
2. ____
3. ____
4. ____
5. ____

CONSUMERIST CHANGE ASSUMPTION

CONSUMERIST CHANGE IMPACT ASSESSMENT

Target market SIC #__________ Industry classification ____________________

or consumer life-style ____________________

I assess at the 90 percent level of confidence that the impact on my target market of the consumerist changes I have assumed on Planning Page 18 will be:

Nature of impact

____

____

____

____

____

Growth strategies that will be affected and how

1. ____
2. ____
3. ____
4. ____
5. ____

VALUE CHANGE ASSUMPTION

VALUE CHANGE IMPACT ASSESSMENT

Target market SIC #__________ Industry classification ____________________

or consumer life-style ____________________

I assess at the 90 percent level of confidence that the impact on my target market of the value changes I have assumed on Planning Page 19 will be:

Nature of impact

Growth strategies that will be affected and how

1. ______________________________
2. ______________________________
3. ______________________________
4. ______________________________
5. ______________________________

GROWTH DEPENDENCY ANALYZER

Potential change areas that must be benign if growth objectives are to be achieved	Specific aspects of every change area on which growth depends
(Check all that apply)	(Write with exactitude)
☐ 1. Economic changes	
☐ 2. Legislative changes	
☐ 3. Market changes	
☐ 4. Technological changes	
☐ 5. Competitive changes	
☐ 6. Management changes	
☐ 7. Labor force changes	
☐ 8. Supply changes	
☐ 9. Consumerist changes	
☐ 10. Value changes	

GROWTH SOURCE CATEGORIZATION AUDIT

Brandable growth categories	Heavy-profit-contributor market(s)
Category 1: New products	
1. ______	SIC #____ ______
2. ______	SIC #____ ______
3. ______	SIC #____ ______
Category 2: Brands	
1. ______	SIC #____ ______
2. ______	SIC #____ ______
3. ______	SIC #____ ______
Category 3: Premature Commodities	
1. ______	SIC #____ ______
2. ______	SIC #____ ______
3. ______	SIC #____ ______
Rebrandable growth category	
Category 4: Mature commodities	
1. ______	SIC #____ ______
2. ______	SIC #____ ______
3. ______	SIC #____ ______

BUSINESS GROWTH OBJECTIVES

SIC #______ Industry classification _________________________

or consumer life-style __________________________

	F19__-F19__ (Year 1)		
	Most likely case	Best case	Worst case
1. Financial objectives			
1.1. Return on growth thrust investment (%)	__	__	__
1.2. Net profit after tax ($000)	$__,___	$__,___	$__,___
1.2.1. Incremental net profit ($000)	$__,___	$__,___	$__,___
1.3. Cash flow ($000)	$__,___	$__,___	$__,___
1.4. Annual earnings growth contribution based on 19__ constant dollars (%)	__	__	__
1.5. Margin over __% average return on total corporate assets (%)	__	__	__
2. Sales objectives			
2.1. Sales volume (#000)	#__,___	#__,___	#__,___
2.2. Sales volume ($000)	$__,___	$__,___	$__,___
2.3. Market share (%)	__	__	__
3. Critical ratios			
3.1. Gross margin (sales/cost of sales)	$__,___	$__,___	$__,___
3.2. Net profit (gross profit/sales)	$__,___	$__,___	$__,___
3.3. Capital turnover times per year (dollar sales volume/investment)	__	__	__

F19__-F19__ (Year 2)			F19__-F19__ (Year 3)		
Most likely case	Best case	Worst case	Most likely case	Best case	Worst case
--	--	--	--	--	--
$--,---	$--,---	$--,---	$--,---	$--,---	$--,---
$--,---	$--,---	$--,---	$--,---	$--,---	$--,---
$--,---	$--,---	$--,---	$--,---	$--,---	$--,---
--	--	--	--	--	--
--	--	--	--	--	--
#--,---	#--,---	#--,---	#--,---	#--,---	#--,---
$--,---	$--,---	$--,---	$--,---	$--,---	$--,---
--	--	--	--	--	--
$--,---	$--,---	$--,---	$--,---	$--,---	$--,---
$--,---	$--,---	$--,---	$--,---	$--,---	$--,---
--	--	--	--	--	--

TOTAL MOST-LIKELY-CASE INCREMENTAL GROWTH OBJECTIVES
(All growth sources)

	F19__-F19__ (Year 1)			
Most likely financial objectives	Total	Cat.1	Cat.2	Cat.3
1.1. Return on growth thrust investment (micro %)		--	--	--
1.2. Net profit after tax ($000)	$--,---	$--,---	$--,---	$--,---
1.3. Cash flow ($000)	$--,---	$--,---	$--,---	$--,---
1.4. Annual earnings growth contribution based on 19__ constant dollars (%)		--	--	--
1.5. Margin over __% average return on total corporate assets (%)		--	--	--

	F19__-F19__ (Year 2)				F19__-F19__ (Year 3)		
otal	Cat.1	Cat.2	Cat.3	Total	Cat.1	Cat.2	Cat.3
	--	--	--		--	--	--
-,---	$--,---	$--,---	$--,---	$--,---	$--,---	$--,---	$--,---
-,---	$--,---	$--,---	$--,---	$--,---	$--,---	$--,---	$--,---
	--	--	--		--	--	--
	--	--	--		--	--	--

GROWTH-OBJECTIVES FORMATION TEAM

	Name	Functional expertise
1.	(Chairman) ________________	____________________
2.	____________________	____________________
3.	____________________	____________________
4.	____________________	____________________
5.	____________________	____________________
6.	____________________	____________________

GROWTH-OBJECTIVES REVIEW AND REVISION TEAM

	Name	Functional expertise
1.	(Chairman) ______	______
2.	______	______
3.	______	______
4.	______	______
5.	______	______
6.	______	______

3

GUIDELINING GROWTH STRATEGIES

There are three preplanning strategies for guidelining growth:

1. Investment intensity guideline
2. Market share guideline
3. Product quality guideline

We judge profit growth according to incremental return on investment. When we set out to accelerate profit, our standard of performance is net incremental return. We define return on investment (ROI) according to the following formula:

$$\text{ROI} = \frac{\text{profit as net pretax income}}{\text{average investment}}$$

By pretax income, we mean profit after expenses but before interest or taxes. By average investment, we mean working capital plus fixed capital employed as assets.

As you look at return on investment in this way, you will be able to see that there are two handles that you can manipulate to improve return. One handle on ROI is to manipulate profit on sales. This can be accomplished in two ways: A higher unit price can be charged or a greater volume of goods can be sold at the same price. The second handle on ROI is to reduce the investment base required to earn new sales revenues or to improve its productivity. This can be accomplished by capital management strategies such as improved inventory levels, improved collections of accounts receivable, reduction of additions to fixed capital, turnarounds and divestments, improved utilization of cash resources, and, of course, reduced borrowing, which can be made possible by generating capital internally.

To accelerate your profit growth, you must pay close attention to your sales income, watch your costs in relation to sales income, and be miserly about the level of capital you employ to earn your sales income. Both the brand-building and the rebranding strategy thrusts we recommend are designed to help you improve sales income. In Appendix 1, you will find a compendium of capital management strategies that can help you reduce your cost base and the level of capital employed in relation to your sales.

Our experience suggests that the most significant constellation of factors conducive to accelerated profit growth is the relationship between volume, costs, and profit. In the management of this three-way mix, the concept of marginal income plays a pivotal role. We define marginal income as sales minus the variable cost of sales. When the marginal income ratio is high, by which we mean at the 40 percent level or better, fixed costs can usually be easily recovered and growth profits can be accumulated readily from even comparatively small increases in volume anywhere above the break-even point. This is so for two reasons. Fixed costs remain the same regardless of increased volume. And after break-even, profit is earned at a much faster rate than sales since marginal income is translated into profit.

The second most significant group of factors in accelerating profit growth is the twinship of volume and price. The optimal profit-making situation is to sell in volume at a branded premium price. If you cannot have volume, you must nonetheless hold premium price. When volume is small, an inverse relationship prevails between volume and price. The smaller the volume, the more important premium price will be in contributing to profit growth.

The three principal guidelines to growth strategies are designed to take into account the interrelationships of volume, cost, price and profit planning. They do so in a way that provides a top management orientation—rather than a functional one such as sales or product engineering—to decide how a growth plan is progressing and if it requires renovation or replanning.

3-1 INVESTMENT INTENSITY

The intensity of your investment in terms of the ratio of your total investment in accelerated growth thrusts to the sales revenues you derive from them. A low investment base and low intensity typically correspond to a high return on investment. The investment intensity guideline is concerned with costs, volume, price and profitability.

3-2 MARKET SHARE

Your percentage market share. Optimal market share is the point at which return on investment is best. Up to this point, return will generally increase with market share. This increase will usually be accompanied by a rising rate of investment turnover and a diminishing ratio of marketing expense to sales. Beyond optimal market share, the point of diminishing return on investment will set in. The market share guideline is principally concerned with volume.

3-3 PRODUCT QUALITY

The quality of your product offering expressed as the sum total of costs invested in a product or system that is being grown at an accelerated rate. The product quality guideline is principally concerned with costs.

Product quality should not be confused with, and is not directly proportional to, a product's utility. Overengineered, overcosted products are often the greatest constraints on high return on investment. An overengineered product is one that suffers from excessive quality; that is, it is capable of delivering a greater benefit or more numerous benefits than its market requires in use or is willing to pay for. You should determine the "enoughness" of the benefits your heavy profit contributors demand and build new brands to its standards or reengineer commodities in conformity with its limits.

A word of warning is necessary. The "enoughness" guideline gives you no permission to manufacture or market nonquality products. What it does mean is that accelerated profit making depends on avoiding dual dangers. One is too little quality, which yields products that cannot be given away. The other is too much quality, which yields products whose costs may not be recoverable. The rule of thumb is to supply enough benefits to command premium price, no more and no less.

These return-on-investment guidelines are intended to serve as useful generalizations for formulating and evaluating your growth strategy thrusts according to proven profit-making principles. Use a separate copy of Planning Page 26 to apply the three ROI guidelines to every brand-building or commodity-rebranding growth thrust as controls against low-return or negative-return growth.

PLANNING PAGE
26

GROWTH EVALUATION GUIDELINES

Business or product: ______________ Sold to SIC #______ Industry classification ______________

or consumer life-style ______________

Check one: ☐ Brand-building thrust ☐ Commodity-rebranding thrust

1. Investment intensity
   (Total investment/sales)

   Optimal investment/sales ratio = __%

   Actual investment/sales ratio = __%

   +/– deviation = __%

2. Market share
   (Percentage penetration/total market)

   Optimal market share (ROI = __%) = __%

   Actual market share (ROI = __%) = __%

   +/– deviation = __%

3. Product quality
   (Sum total of costs invested)

   Optimal product quality (cost) = $__,___,___

   Actual product quality (cost) = $__,___,___

   +/– deviation = $__,___,___

GROWTH EVALUATION GUIDELINES

Business or product: ________ Sold to SIC #_____ Industry classification ________

or consumer life-style ________

Check one: ☐ Brand-building thrust ☐ Commodity-rebranding thrust

1. Investment intensity
   (Total investment/sales)

   Optimal investment/sales ratio = __%

   Actual investment/sales ratio = __%

   +/- deviation = __%

2. Market share
   (Percentage penetration/total market)

   Optimal market share (ROI = __%) = __%

   Actual market share (ROI = __%) = __%

   +/- deviation = __%

3. Product quality
   (Sum total of costs invested)

   Optimal product quality (cost) = $__,___,___

   Actual product quality (cost) = $__,___,___

   +/- deviation = $__,___,___

GROWTH EVALUATION GUIDELINES

Business or product: ______________ Sold to SIC #______ Industry classification ______________

or consumer life-style ______________

Check one: ☐ Brand-building thrust ☐ Commodity-rebranding thrust

1. Investment intensity
   (Total investment/sales)

   Optimal investment/sales ratio = __%

   Actual investment/sales ratio = __%

   +/- deviation = __%

2. Market share
   (Percentage penetration/total market)

   Optimal market share (ROI = __%) = __%

   Actual market share (ROI = __%) = __%

   +/- deviation = __%

3. Product quality
   (Sum total of costs invested)

   Optimal product quality (cost) = $__,___,___

   Actual product quality (cost) = $__,___,___

   +/- deviation = $__,___,___

GROWTH EVALUATION GUIDELINES

Business or product: ______________ Sold to SIC #______ Industry classification ______________
or consumer life-style ______________

Check one: ☐ Brand-building thrust ☐ Commodity-rebranding thrust

1. Investment intensity
   (Total investment/sales)

   Optimal investment/sales ratio = --%

   Actual investment/sales ratio = --%

   +/- deviation = --%

2. Market share
   (Percentage penetration/total market)

   Optimal market share (ROI = --%) = --%

   Actual market share (ROI = --%) = --%

   +/- deviation = --%

3. Product quality
   (Sum total of costs invested)

   Optimal product quality (cost) = $--,---,---

   Actual product quality (cost) = $--,---,---

   +/- deviation = $--,---,---

PART TWO

GROWTH PLANNING

4

BRAND-BUILDING STRATEGY THRUSTS

There are six growth-planning strategies for building brands:

1. Branded-business positioning
2. Market value alignment
3. Marketcentered business organization
4. Brand pricing
5. High-awareness/positive-attitude advertising
6. Brand-family proliferation

Brand-building strategy thrusts are designed to be applied to three categories of businesses or products: new products, existing brands, and premature commodities.

Category 1: New Products

New products, which we place in Category 1, are sometimes brand candidates. If they win market acceptance, they will become brands. Brandedness is the key to premium profit making because only brands command the premium price that permits premium profits to be earned. To accelerate profit growth, new products with brand capability must be moved to a positive cash-flow position as quickly as possible.

You can manufacture a new product with branded capability, but a market is the sole authority that can confer brand status on it. In this sense, markets and not manufacturers make brands. It is a market's perception of premium value in a new product that endows it with brandedness. It is a market's willingness, even eagerness in many cases, to pay a premium price to obtain the premium value it perceives that enables a brand to be a big profit winner.

If a market votes down a new product's candidacy for brandedness, the product will become a premature commodity if it is able to survive at all. Because not all new products are automatic brands, it is best to regard them only as alleged brands until they pass beyond their break points. It is also best to regard their benefit values as alleged values until these have been validated by market acceptance. Up to that point, it is the better part of wisdom to maintain that new products have only an assumed market.

Brand-building strategy thrusts for new products should be directed to accelerating their growth through breakeven so that they can achieve brandedness in the shortest time. Once the products become brands, some of the same strategy thrusts can be used to continue to drive them upward at an enhanced rate. If you set about to accelerate the growth of a brand that you have managed to brandedness from its inception, the foundation work of marketcentering the product's organization structure and aligning the product with its market's value system will already have been done. You will therefore be able to concentrate on the minimal number of strategies required to accelerate the brand's market penetration.

Category 2: Brands

Brands are Category 2 for growth planning. Products in this category have a leading competitive position in a market that they serve with a perceived preemptive benefit. The single overriding clue to brandedness is the ability to command premium price. Products that enjoy this profit-making advantage are known by different terms in industry: specialty products, proprietary products, or performance products. Whatever their nomenclature, they are brands if they are commanders of premium price.

A brand is a product that has captured a market's perception of preemptively high value in relation to price. This makes it a mighty profit-making machine. Because its profit per unit of sale is high, it is capable of producing earnings at a rate that can be far in excess of the rate of sales. It can seize and hold leadership in its market and act as the standard of value against which all competitive offerings must be unsuccessfully evaluated. It can become franchised by a market, quite literally being licensed to conduct business with the market on the most preferential terms.

Every company, every division, and every department must have a going brand in its product mix if it is to stand a chance of accumulating the significant profits that generate internal capital.

Category 3: Premature Commodities

Category 3 contains new products that have not won election as brands. They are prematurely commodities. Some can be repositioned into brands. Other new products such as many line extensions are conceived from their origin as commodities. They make their market entry as commodities and remain commodities throughout their life cycles. Many premature commodities cannot be branded because they lack perceived preemptive value. They are acceptable to their markets but have not been made preferable to them.

How to Tell If You Have a Brand or a Brand Candidate

A brand or a brandable new product is a product whose earnings are still growing and have yet to peak. A minimum sales growth of 2 times the rate of growth of the gross national product or at least continuous, steady market expansion is occurring. A brand's high perceived value/price ratio permits high unit profits to accrue. These profits are immediately consumed by reinvestment during a brand's early life.

Brand management tends to be entrepreneurial. It is market-sensitive. In response to market needs, proliferations of the original brand may be brought out to create a product family under the brand's trade name.

Users of a brand perceive it as possessing the ability to confer a proprietary, differentiated benefit. They endow it with specialty status. This leads to the single most important attribute of a brand: *it can command a premium price, yet because of its perceived premium value it is nonetheless positioned as a bargain.*

A brand may have no direct competition. If rivals exist, there may be a single major competitor or, at most, two. They will not simply be competing for market share against each other. Their competition will be against a lack of market awareness of the brand's generic benefits or the absence of a positive attitude toward them. Once customers perceive a brand's value, they ask questions that begin with the word "when" with which they initiate inquiries about time of delivery and availability of special features.

If you have a consumer product, your sales strategies will center on benefit-type advertising calculated to obtain high awareness and build positive attitudes toward the brand's preemptive value. If you have an industrial product, you will be doing the majority of your business on the 2:2, 2:1 and 1:1, 1:2 basis shown as Brand Country in Exhibit 1-2.

Six Strategy Thrusts

There are six basic strategy thrusts that you can mix and match to accelerate the growth of brands, new products, and premature commodities:

1. Branded-business positioning
2. Market value alignment
3. Marketcentered business organization
4. Brand pricing
5. High-awareness/positive-attitude advertising
6. Brand-family proliferation

Not all brands or brandable candidates will require all six thrusts. The mix and match will be different almost every time. Even if the elements are not different, their allocated emphasis will be. The best rule to follow is to tailor every growth thrust to its minimal requirements so that you can ensure cost-effective brand building.

4-1 BRANDED-BUSINESS POSITIONING

Business positioning is market need alignment. For every target market in which a branded business is planned for growth at an accelerated rate, the business must be positioned in line with the single most crucial benefit that the brand can confer on its heavy profit contributors. Brand marketing strategy is the sum total of all forms of promotion of this "net benefit."

The business position that you reach for a brand in every growth market will be the ultimate determinant of the brand's ability to accelerate profit. This is true for a simple reason: the brand's position becomes your *business definition.* As such, it will be the main attraction for your heavy profit contributors.

Use a separate copy of Planning Page 27 to pair your brand's single most crucial benefit with every target market's single most crucial need. This pairing will become the crux of your brand growth formula. On the basis of every brand benefit–market need pairing, use a separate copy of Planning Page 28 to position the brand's business in every target market.

The positioning statement shown on Planning Page 28 is target market–oriented. It seeks to relate a brand's business immediately to the prime need of its target of heavy profit contributors. It then relates this need to the prime benefit which the brand can provide for them and to the technological capabilities from which the brand's benefit in use is derived. Finally, the positioning statement relates the brand to its competition.

A brand's beneficial positioning *is* the brand in its market's perceptions. Positioning is what is marketable about a branded business. It is the central fact in its growth thrust.

4-2 MARKET VALUE ALIGNMENT

Accelerated growth planning requires a 1:1 congruency of the values of a business with the values of its heavy-profit-contributor market.

One value to consider carefully is the perceived value of size and diversity. To be the biggest business with the broadest product line may be a negative value in terms of a market's reaction to bigness or its attitude toward conglomerate diversity. The largest staff, the deepest inventories, and the widest range of products are still values in many markets. But in others they are losing their preferred status to the specialist: the one-business supplier who is perceived to know everything there is to know about a single product or system and whose business is not distracted by other interests.

Other values that should be considered in relation to their ability to support a growth thrust are the degree and type of competitiveness favored by a target market, market reaction to instilling high technology into a product line or preference for simplistic, less costly, and perhaps less troublesome products, and the use of certain raw materials, ingredients or energy sources whose origins or effects may be identified with negative political, economic, or social values. Since negative value attributions can impede or completely thwart accelerated growth thrusts, you must be certain to eradicate any "pernicious contraries" from the values that a growth business projects.

Planning Page 29 is a matrix that enables you to make an inventory of the current values with which you must align in your target markets. Use a separate copy of the planning page to describe the effects on every target market that every change area across the top of the matrix can have on the market value categories shown in the vertical column. (You have already made assumptions in Section 2-3 of Chapter 2 about the impact you anticipate from the change areas shown on the matrix.) Then use a separate copy of Planning Page 30 to summarize the responsive actions that you must take in every target market to align your growth thrusts with the values which can encourage acceleration.

4-3 MARKETCENTERED BUSINESS ORGANIZATION

Commodity-based businesses typically operate from three types of organization base: (1) materials centering, by which a business is centered on a raw material such as a plastics division, a paperboard division, and a metals division of a packaging company; (2) product centering, by which a business is centered on a product or product group such as the Chevrolet Division or a building products department; or (3) process centering, by which a business is centered on a technical process such as an extruded plastics division, a pressed steel division, or a data processing department.

A branded business must reject these traditional organization formats if its growth is to be accelerated. It should be centered not on materials, products, or processes but on its heavy-profit-contributor market: a personal care market, for example, or a home repair market, a nuclear energy market, or a securities-trading market.

Marketcentering a brand business brings two significant advantages. First, it is the best way to inject an acute sensitivity to market needs into the business. Second, it is the best way to make sure that marketing and R&D interface tightly so that market signals can be utilized as pathfinders for the development functions, analyzing the direction in which market needs and materials and energy availability are pointing and then prescribing optional branded-product vehicles to help move in the same way.

Under marketcentering, a broad range of branded products and services can be centered on the needs of a target market in a highly concentrated manner. When such a marketcentered organization at the division or department level is correlated with centralized corporate services for control and consultation, the resulting structure can combine the best of both worlds: extreme tiptoe flexibility at the operating points of contact with the market coupled with consistency of policy and dependability of service support at the top.

There are several forms of organization that can make a group of heavy-profit-contributor customer needs the center of a business. IBM's data processing operations are segmented organizationally according to key markets, such as institutions like hospitals and retail establishments like supermarkets. General Foods has adopted a market-targeting organization style based on strategic business units. Even the strict product orientation of some scientific companies can be converted to a combined product and market orientation built around "customer provinces." In its electronics product marketing, for example, Hewlett-Packard has created a sales and service group that concentrates separately on the electrical manufacturing market while another group serves the market for aerospace. Still other groups sell to the markets for communications or transportation equipment.

General Electric has structured strategic business groups for its major appliance and power generation businesses. For GE, the process of reorganizing from a product to a market orientation has been especially difficult. An average department contains 3½ product lines and may serve more than one business or, more frequently, only a part of a major business. Electric motors, for example, are divided among eight departments. Home refrigerators are split between two departments, even though the only significant product difference is the way in which the doors open.

In other companies, similar steps have been taken to orient businesses to their markets. At Mead, broad market clusters have been organized to serve customer needs in home building and furnishings, education, and leisure. PPG Industries has been examining the benefits of systemizing the marketing of its paint, ceramics, and glass divisions through a home environment profit center whose product mix could resemble the pattern shown in Exhibit 4-1. Monsanto has organized a fire safety center that consolidates fire safety products from every sector of Monsanto and groups them according to the markets they serve: building and construction, transportation, apparel, or furnishings. Revlon has been engaged in "breaking up the company into little pieces." It has created as many as six autonomous profit centers, each of which is designed to serve a specific market segment.

EXHIBIT 4-1

MODEL MULTIPRODUCT MARKETCENTER

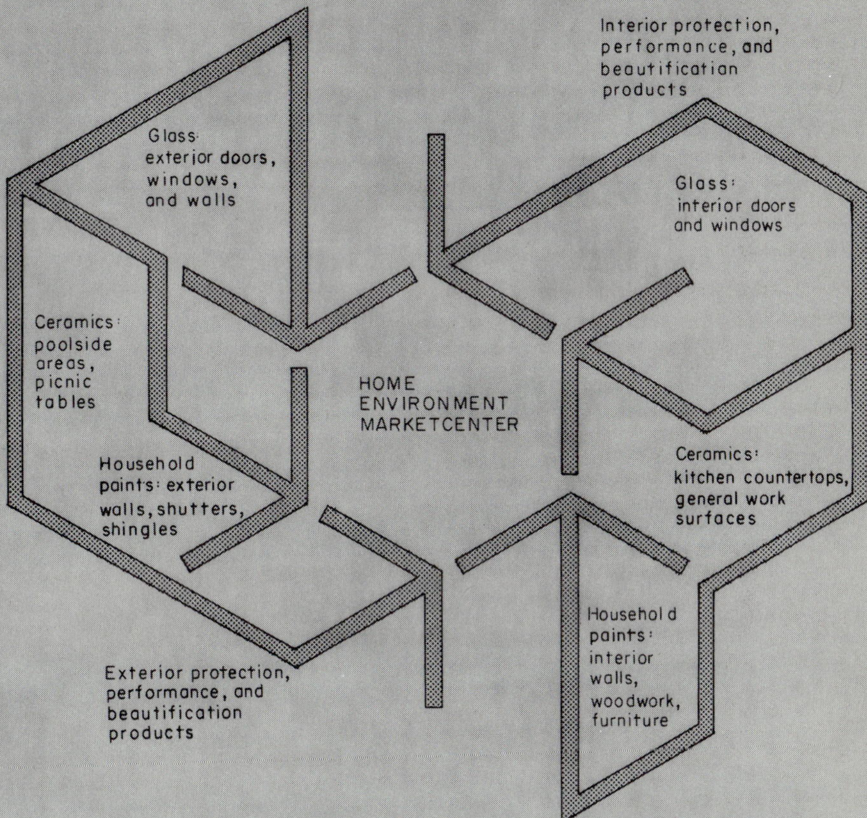

Marketcentering describes the way in which progressive banks are organizing "financial needs groups" to serve the specific financing needs of manufacturers of electronic systems, drugs, cosmetics, household products, and other major product categories. Marketcentering also describes the way in which some railroads are grouping their services around the common distribution needs of major customers so that they can provide a branded user-oriented service system for oil, chemical, and fertilizer shippers and a different but also branded system for grain shippers.

When an organization is marketcentered, a heavy-profit-contributor market becomes its focal point. The objective of the business is to become its market's preferred center for fulfilling one or more principal needs. The marketcenter must define its market according to a system of its closely related needs. This permits the market to be served by a single brand or a diversified package of brands and commodity products and services that, taken together, supply a combination of closely related benefits. The business may market two or more related products in a single sale or market a package composed of products and their related services.

Exhibits 4-2A through 4-2C show three optional stages in the progressive marketcentering of a high-technology company that originally regarded its mission as serving three markets: an industrial market, an institutional market (primarily government), and original equipment manufacturers (OEM). Option A shows an organization structure based on these three markets supported by a central core of technical, financial, and marketing services. A specialized tech group has been assigned to the industrial marketcenter to serve a current exotic need. In Option B, the three marketcenters have been consolidated. The OEM center is positioned here as a segment of the industrial market, not as a separate market in itself. The specialized tech group has been absorbed into the central service core.

Option C shows the ultimate segmentation of the marketcenters, a sophisticated culmination to the progressive centering process. Each segment has its own business manager. The OEM subsegment in every industrial market is incorporated within the industry marketcenter. When necessary, a separate OEM business manager can run it. The three segments in the institutional marketcenter group can represent federal, state, and local government markets, or they can be organized as one overall government segment and two industrial markets.

Because a marketcenter is operated as a profit center, it should be administered by an entrepreneurial *business manager*. A business manager is fully profit-responsible. The manager should enjoy considerable authority, including the right to set prices and control costs, and should also be empowered to make all other decisions necessary to operate the marketcenter for superior profit. Business managers are the chief line officers

EXHIBIT 4-2A

OPTION A

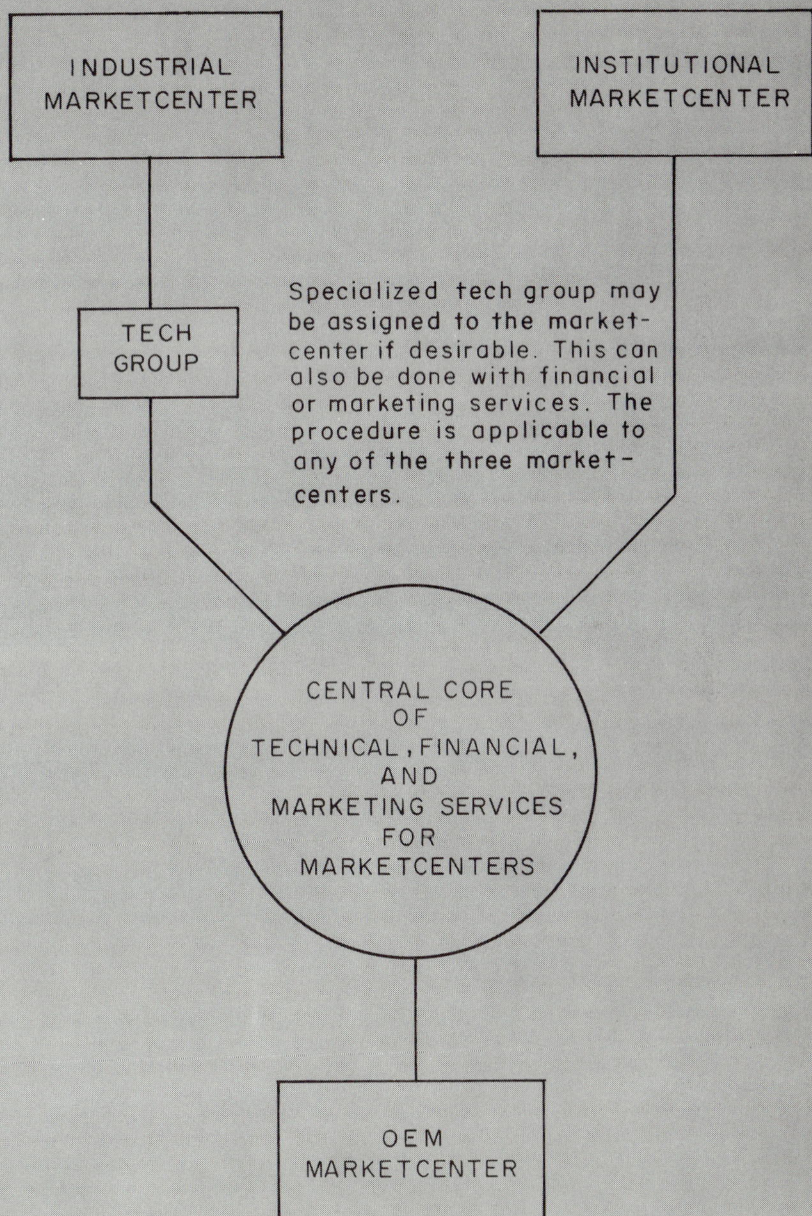

EXHIBIT 4-2B

OPTION B

Move from three Marketcenters to two.

Consider OEM as a specialized industrial market, or subsegment.

Correlate OEM and industrial marketing strategies closely.

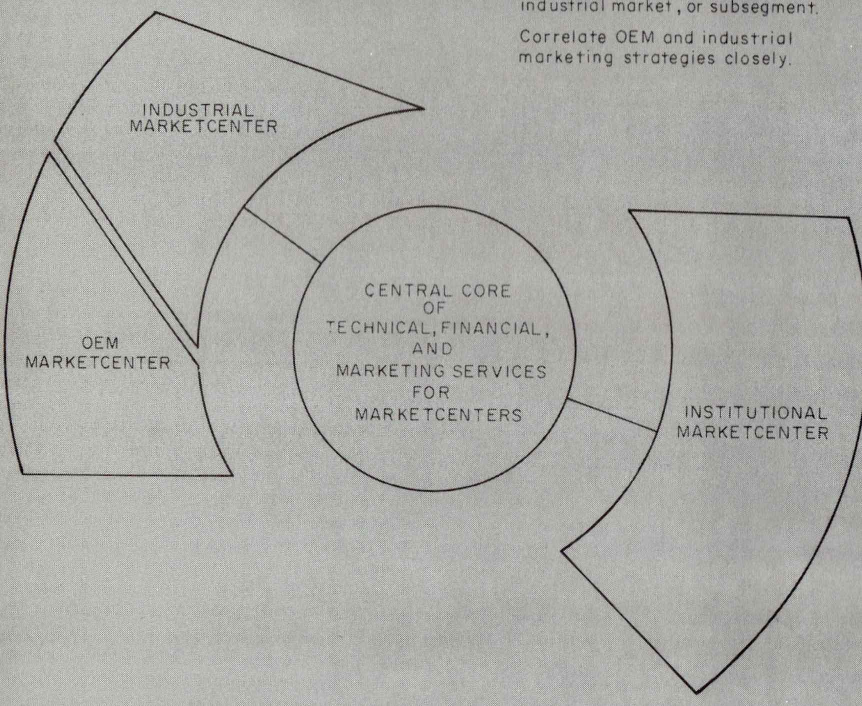

EXHIBIT 4-2C

OPTION C

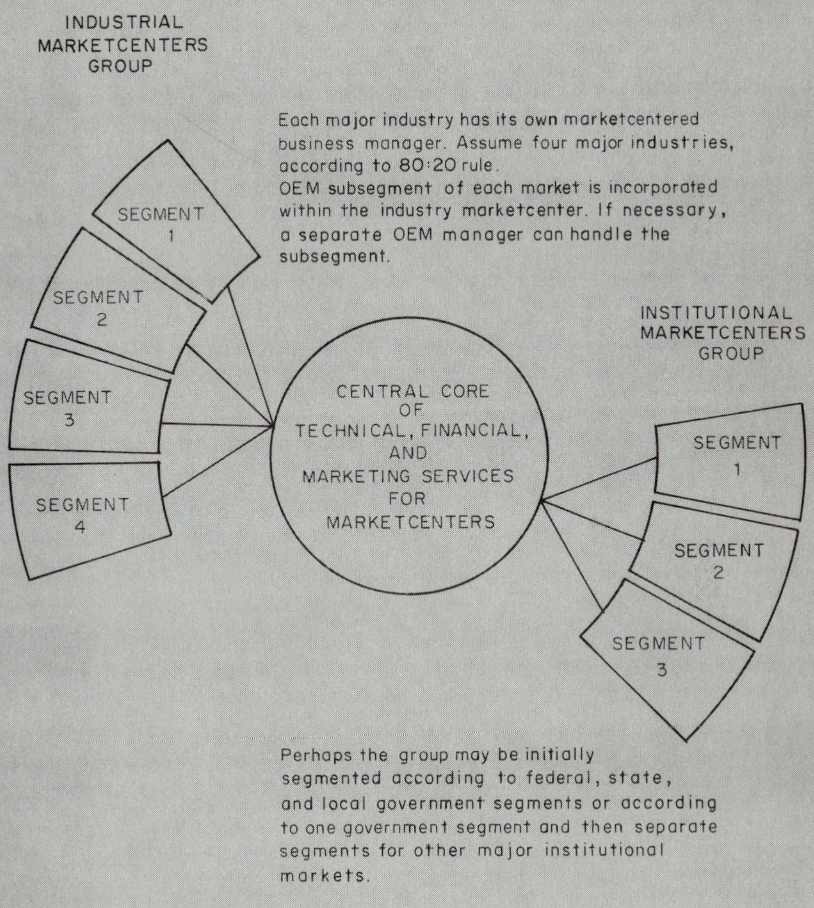

in their marketcentered organizations. All other functions must be repositioned as satellite supply services that support the business managers' operations. Business managers may have the right to employ division or corporate staff services on a contractual basis. This gives them authority to refuse to do business with any internal service that cannot be competitive with external services in pricing, quality control, or delivery. Exhibit 4-3 shows a typical business manager's internal interrelationships.

Once a business is marketcentered, its storehouse of information about its target market quickly becomes its key asset. Through marketcentering, a business can grow at an accelerated rate by basing its future expansion on knowledge about the needs of its existing markets.

Top corporate or division management must position itself as a holding company or, as the function is sometimes called, a central banker for its marketcenters. The central banker acts as a council of portfolio managers who centralize corporate policy making and investment funding for their marketcentered businesses.

If you plan to marketcenter a brand's organization structure and operations, refer to Exhibit 4-1 as a model. Use Planning Page 31 to center the brand's business on its heavy-profit-contributor market. Define the market according to its single most crucial need. Then refer to Exhibit 4-3 so that you can use Planning Page 32 as an organization chart to assign a business manager and support services to managing the marketcenter. Use separate copies of each of these planning pages for every marketcenter you plan.

4-4 BRAND PRICING

A brand is known by the price it keeps. The single most significant test of brandedness is the ability to command a premium price.

Brand pricing is justified as premium pricing because a brand's perceived value is a premium value. Brand price should therefore be maximum price; that is, it should be set as high as its perceived value will permit. Brand price should have no relation to a product's cost base except to exceed it by the greatest possible margin.

The plastics industry provides a dramatic but not by any means unusual example of the discrepancy between brand pricing at premium levels and commodity pricing. In the mid-1970s high-performance polymers, a subsegment of engineering polymers, were able to command a price range that topped out at $1 per cubic inch (16.4 cubic centimeters). At the same time, commodity plastics such as polypropylene, polyethylene, and polystyrene could ask only 1.5 cents per cubic inch at the top of their price range. In this case, the value added to the manufacturer by branding was 98.5 cents, or almost a 100:1 difference.

It is not so much that a brand *can* bear a premium price because it offers premium value. A brand *must* bear a premium price if it is to be brandable

EXHIBIT 4-3

BUSINESS MANAGER INTERFACES

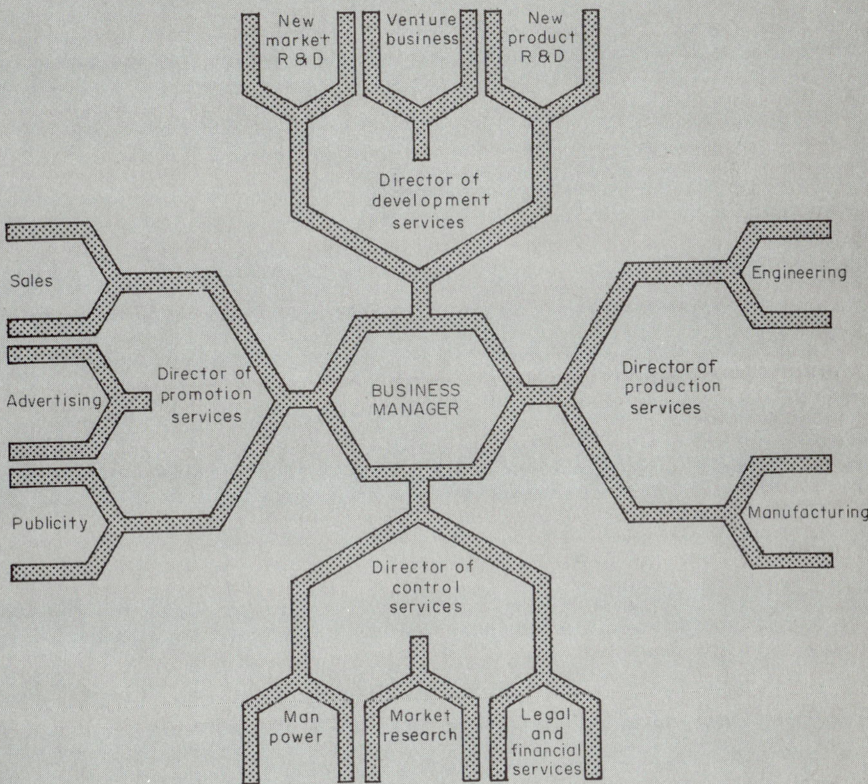

in the perception of its market. All value lies in market perception. There is no implicit value in a product's physical or chemical components unless they can be translated into perceived benefits. Otherwise, components and ingredients are merely costs. Prices based on costs are commodity prices.

A brand's formula can be reduced to a simple equation: perceived value exceeds price, or $PV > P$. This formula for a brand is the formula for a bargain. A bargain is a product whose value exceeds its price. No matter how high a bargain's price may be, its perceived value is greater.

Brand pricing is return-on-investment pricing. As long as the return is greater than the investment (which includes the price), the basis exists for a fair deal.

Brand pricing has two functions. One is a marketing function that favors the user. The other is a financial function that favors the supplier. The marketing function of a brand's premium price is to signal to its users the advent of premium value even before their actual experience of purchase and use. Brand price is a key marketing clue that predocuments value. This enables the purchase to be made comfortably. It also permits eventual product use to confirm the expectation engendered by premium price that a premium value will be conferred.

The financial function of premium price is to generate premium profits. The cash flow created by this stream of profit has several uses. First and foremost, it can support the brand's accelerated sales growth. It can also be employed to pay back the sunk costs underlying the brand's investment. It can pay back some or all of the costs of developing unrelated new products or proliferating closely related line extensions in the brand's family. It can support the financing of new business ventures, the turnaround of premature commodities, and the rebranding of mature commodities.

For most companies, the majority of their cash flow is brand cash flow. Sometimes the majority of cash flow will be generated by a mature commodity. But most often it is brand sales that yield the greatest cash flow. We think of cash flow as net income after taxes, plus some noncash charges such as depreciation. It is frequently expressed in the form of retained earnings.

Brand-pricing strategy is to maximize cash flow. Planning Page 33 shows a format for correlating cash flow and brand-pricing strategy on a quarter-by-quarter basis. Use a separate copy of the planning page to calculate the cash flows that can most likely be generated at various price levels in every target market.

4-5 HIGH-AWARENESS/POSITIVE-ATTITUDE ADVERTISING

Advertising is a multiplier of perceived value. Its role in branded growth acceleration is twofold. It must multiply the rate at which a brand's heavy profit contributors become aware of the brand's single most crucial benefit. It must then multiply the strength and conviction of the positive attitudes that they develop toward acquiring the benefit.

High market awareness is the result of three factors:

1. A valuable benefit to be aware of so that attention and interest in the brand's proposition are justified
2. A memorable and credible presentation of the benefit so that it sticks in consciousness despite competitive attrition
3. A frequent-enough repetition of the benefit so that a sufficient "blood level" can be maintained in a sufficient percentage of the brand's heavy-profit-contributor market

In creating high-awareness advertising, the three major constraints to be overcome are the inertial indifference of a market, its selective inattention in the midst of many competitive distractions and other compulsions, and its imprecise differentiation between one brand's benefit and competitive benefits.

Awareness always creates an attitude. The resulting attitude can be either positive or negative. The mere fact of awareness is no guarantee of a positive attitude. High awareness of many products is accompanied by negative attitudes. This is why awareness itself is only one-half of the brand advertising equation. The other half is positive-attitude building.

There are two levels of positive attitude. The base level is acceptance. When heavy profit contributors accept a brand's single most crucial benefit, the brand can become competitive. This will put it in business. But simply putting a brand in business is not enough. Acceptance will rarely provide sufficient acceleration for growth. To grow at a superior rate, a brand must strive for the higher level of positive attitude called "preference." When heavy profit contributors prefer a brand's single most crucial benefit, they will isolate it from competition so that it can achieve a transient monopoly. It will temporarily monopolize preference.

High preference is a result of two factors:

1. A superior positioning of a branded benefit so that it is perceived to best satisfy market needs
2. A superior rationale for acquiring the benefit that will prevent or relieve anxiety, justify action, and make the transaction appear to be comfortable even before it has taken place.

In creating high-preference advertising, the three major constraints to be overcome are preexisting preferences already established in the attitudes of prospective heavy profit contributors, the profit contributors' failure to perceive the value/price ratio of the benefit to be superior to their accustomed benefits, and their reluctance to change to a new, unfamiliar source of supply.

Preference must be instilled by advertising so that purchase can occur. Preference must precede purchase. Otherwise, buying will not take place. The actual product experience that follows purchase must confirm the preference that preceded it. In this sense, purchase validates preference and reinforces it so that repeat purchases can follow.

Use a separate set of Planning Pages 34 and 35 to work out the factors in your brand-building advertising plan that can create high awareness of your brand's single most crucial benefit and a high positive attitude toward acquiring it in every one of your heavy-profit-contributor markets.

4-6 BRAND-FAMILY PROLIFERATION

Brand consolidation in a target market is an invitation to brand proliferation in the same market or into adjacent markets.

The original big-winner brand can act as the progenitor of a brand family of products or businesses based on the same general branded benefit. A brand's family can be composed of extended products that replicate the branded benefit in new shapes, sizes, colors, consistencies, flavors, textures, or capacities. By further extension into closely related businesses, the branded benefit can also be replicated in the form of new venture businesses that serve adjacent market segments and thereby proliferate the brand's penetration.

Brand product families such as the "Ford family of fine cars" and *brand business families* such as Gerber baby foods and Gerber family insurance serve several purposes. One is to add new sources of profitable sales volume. Another is to protect a market and prepare to defend it against competition along a broad front. A third purpose is to spread manufacturing and marketing costs such as sales and advertising over a wide base as a means of reducing waste coverage and achieving greater cost effectiveness.

Brand Product-Family Proliferation

Use a separate copy of Planning Page 36 to plan the proliferation of an existing brand into a new market or to plan the brand's line extension into its current market segment.

Brand Business-Family Proliferation[1]

New branded businesses are the correlates of new branded products. They offer the same advantages of capital generation through premium pricing. Like branded-product proliferation, branded-business ventures that take off from an established brand must be based on the brand formula: the perceived premium value from dealing with the business must exceed the premium price that has to be paid.

The added growth value of venture business proliferation is not due principally to diversity, although diversification may offer countercyclical earning opportunities. Diversification's major contribution to accelerated growth is the new ability that it offers to penetrate target markets of awakening opportunity by catching their curves when they are on the rise.

Brandable-business proliferation can be accomplished through either of two types of venture:

1. New enterprise development, either alone or as a joint venturer on a 50:50 shared-investment–shared-risk basis
2. Foothold acquisition, either partially as a minority investor or through outright purchase

New Enterprise Development

To be most cost-effective, a new developmental enterprise should be a process of logical extension from an existing brand franchise. At the very outset of a commitment to venture, you should answer two questions that will help predict a venture's format and business positioning:

1. What is the branded base of assets, both technical and in the market, from which we can grow a business?
2. What extensions from our base are most logical in terms of their utilization of these assets?

For a branded-business proliferation to qualify as being venturable, a small, select list of standards must be met. You should be able to say something like this: "Given our branded base for growth, we can sensibly expect that our venture will be able to exceed a 30 percent pretax return on funds expended and will be able to generate a minimum of 20 percent pretax return on total investment. We can also anticipate that our capability and opportunity mix will permit our venture to establish an annual rate of $20 million in net sales by the end of the venture's fifth year of commercial life. Beginning from that point in time, we also have a right to

[1] A more detailed treatment of this subject can be found in Mack Hanan, *Venture Management*, McGraw-Hill Book Company, New York, 1976.

anticipate a break-even position by Year 3 and a minimum 8 percent annual rate of profit growth through at least Year 5. No ventures that cannot promise to meet these expectations will be considered since they will not be capitalizing fully enough on our branded base of opportunity and capability."

The objective of a venture selection process ought to be to spot winners, not to avoid losers. The selection process must help ensure that the one potential big winner out of every ten or so candidates is identified before it can slip away. Using a selection process to screen in the elusive big winners rather than to screen out future failures gives a positive approach to venture development. It allies venture selection to your venture objectives, which must be to seek out and commercialize profitable new businesses rather than to build an inventory of unprofitable ones. It can achieve an additional benefit, too, in deterring venture managers from trying to beat the 9:1 odds against success by providing a tool for operating within the odds and making them work to advantage. It teaches them that the major risks in venturing are never those posed by total losses, break-even businesses, or marginally profitable businesses. The unaffordable risk is the big winner that is not ventured.

Venture winners are generally rated according to their return on investment. This relegates their gross sales dollar volume, rate of annual sales growth, percentage share of market, and total marketing investment to subsidiary status as success criteria. Other companion objectives to ROI can include increased earnings per share for the venture's parent company above the so-called good average of 8 to 9 percent, improved dividends and appreciation of net worth, growth of capital, and return on shareholders' equity.

Use a separate copy of Planning Page 37 to position every venture business. Then use copies of Planning Page 38 to work out the venture's objectives. If you plan to venture jointly with another department or division or with another company, use separate copies of Planning Pages 39 and 40.

Foothold Acquisition

Acquisition of someone else's branded or brandable business can be a quick substitute for venturing on your own. Instead of funding a start-up venture business, by means of an acquisition you can market a going concern's products immediately. You will inherit the growth positioning of any business you acquire. This includes its premium-pricing capability.

There are two types of acquisition, minority investment in smaller companies or foothold acquisition through majority investment or buy-out. Minority investment is a cooperative format for acquisition. One company, usually the larger one, makes an investment of less than 50 percent in a smaller or younger company. As a rule, the investor will seek to control between 20 and 45 percent of each company whose growth it sponsors in its role as a minority venture capitalist.

A minority-interest investment can have one of three objectives. It can be a learning experience, enabling a company to test on a small scale what it would be like to be in a new business: what the technological requirements are or what the marketing problems can be. Investment in this case is the same as financing a continuing market research project. Second, a minority investment can represent a foothold acquisition possibility. Finally, it can represent a short-term investment opportunity that may result in taking the sponsored business into public ownership. In this last instance, the investment is similar to a loan.

While ground rules vary among minority investing companies, almost all of them look for certain characteristics in a venture investment. Typically, a gain of 5 times the initial investment over a 2-to-3-year period, with a 10-times gain over 3 to 4 years, is desired. Within 3 to 5 years, a normally expected return on investment is 20 percent. A minimum patience time of 3 to 5 years will probably be required for most investment situations.

At the point at which the initial investment has grown 10 times, buy-out may be an option. If it is exercised, the company can then be merged into the investing corporation as a new department or as part of an existing division or be managed as a subsidiary.

Small private companies in an early developmental stage of growth, but still lacking an assured, long-term income-generating capability or broad market acceptance, are among the best prospects for investment.

An investing company's interest may be expressed initially in the form of a client-consultant relationship. The company can then move to the private investment stage. A usual investment ranges from as little as $50,000 to $1 million or more. Sometimes an independent venture capital investor is invited to become a third party to the deal. In such cases, the venture becomes a three-legged stool on which the investing corporation, the outside investors, and the venture principals all sit in minority positions.

While minority-investment acquisitions are buy-ins, foothold acquisitions are buy-outs. An independent company, preferably small and possessing an established product-line system, can be purchased to give the acquiring company an immediate foothold. Market entry is assured. The start-up costs and many time lags associated with internal development may be avoided. In this way, foothold acquisitions or their smaller versions, toehold acquisitions, may represent a simplified means of entering new business areas in high-growth fields.

A foothold acquisition made as a venture should be undertaken for operational reasons and not simply for short-term financial benefits. Generally, it represents a trade-off. On the one hand, there are the emotional and dollar values of the acquiring company's desire to get into a new business quickly and surely. On the other hand, there is the cost of buying someone else's successful experience. Another major consideration is the cost effectiveness of the acquiring company's R&D function, which sets a floor for make-or-buy decisions.

Acquisition criteria vary significantly. Some selection standards are nevertheless fairly well agreed on. First, foothold acquisitions should be in businesses that the acquirer knows something about. This means that they should be more or less natural extensions. Second, an acquired company must have proved management that is willing to stay on. Third, an acquired company should not dilute the acquirer's earnings.

Several other criteria are also common. A foothold's size should be large enough to provide all the necessary operating skills in sufficient depth so that it can continue to operate successfully without major intervention from the acquiring company. The foothold should also be well enough established to have strong industry contacts and customer relationships. It ought not to be so large, however, that it dominates its industry. No major parts of the foothold's business should be outside the acquirer's area of interest. If they are, their subsequent spin-off should be relatively well assured beforehand.

Most acquiring companies prefer acquisitions that offer the opportunity to increase their profits per share within a reasonably short period. Some acquirers also seek acquisitions whose capability base can put them into more than one industry segment or life-styled market. Almost without exception, acquirers insist on compatibility: a reputation with key trade, professional, and customer groups that is comfortably in keeping with the acquiring company's self-image. Furthermore, the acquisition's key people should be compatible with the acquirer's key people.

Use a separate copy of Planning Page 41 to position an acquisition business. Then use copies of Planning Page 42 to work out the acquisition's objectives.

PLANNING PAGES
27–42

BRANDED BUSINESS POSITIONING PLAN

Branded business name: ______________________________

Target Market SIC #______ Industry classification ____________

or consumer life-style ____________

Heavy-profit-contributor market's single most crucial need	Brand's single most preferred benefit to satisfy single most crucial need

BRANDED BUSINESS POSITIONING STATEMENT

SIC #______ Industry classification ____________________

or consumer life-style ____________________

1. The (branded business name) ____________________ is in business to preempt satisfaction of the heavy-profit-contributor market segment's single most crucial need for

____

____

2. To solve the market's major problem of (nature of problem and the operating process, function, or use pattern that it affects) ____________________________________

____

3. By applying the benefits of:

3.1. ____________________________________

3.2. ____________________________________

3.3. ____________________________________

4. Which we deliver through (products, services, or systems):

4.1. ____________________________________

4.2. ____________________________________

4.3. ____________________________________

5. Derived from the technological capabilities of:

5.1. ____________________________________

5.2. ____________________________________

6. Marketed against the competition of:

Direct competition	Indirect competition
6.1. ______________	6.1. ______________
6.2. ______________	6.2. ______________
6.3. ______________	6.3. ______________

BRANDED BUSINESS POSITIONING PLAN

Branded business name: ______________________________

Target Market SIC #______ Industry classification __________

or consumer life-style __________

Heavy-profit-contributor market's single most crucial need	Brand's single most preferred benefit to satisfy single most crucial need

BRANDED BUSINESS POSITIONING STATEMENT

SIC #______ Industry classification ____________________

or consumer life-style ____________________

1. The (branded business name) ____________________
   is in business to preempt satisfaction of the heavy-profit-contributor market segment's single most crucial need for

   ____

   ____

2. To solve the market's major problem of (nature of problem and the operating process, function, or use pattern that it affects) ____________________

   ____

3. By applying the benefits of:

   3.1. ______________________________

   3.2. ______________________________

   3.3. ______________________________

4. Which we deliver through (products, services, or systems):

   4.1. ______________________________

   4.2. ______________________________

   4.3. ______________________________

5. Derived from the technological capabilities of:

   5.1. ______________________________

   5.2. ______________________________

6. Marketed against the competition of:

<u>Direct competition</u>	<u>Indirect competition</u>
6.1. ________________	6.1. ________________
6.2. ________________	6.2. ________________
6.3. ________________	6.3. ________________

BRANDED BUSINESS POSITIONING PLAN

Branded business name: ______________________________

Target Market SIC #______ Industry classification __________

or consumer life-style __________

Heavy-profit-contributor market's single most crucial need	Brand's single most preferred benefit to satisfy single most crucial need

BRANDED BUSINESS POSITIONING STATEMENT

SIC #_______ Industry classification ____________________

or consumer life-style ____________________

1. The (branded business name) ____________________ is in business to preempt satisfaction of the heavy-profit-contributor market segment's single most crucial need for·

____

____

2. To solve the market's major problem of (nature of problem and the operating process, function, or use pattern that it affects) ____________________

____

3. By applying the benefits of:

   3.1. ____________________

   3.2. ____________________

   3.3. ____________________

4. Which we deliver through (products, services, or systems):

   4.1. ____________________

   4.2. ____________________

   4.3. ____________________

5. Derived from the technological capabilities of:

   5.1. ____________________

   5.2. ____________________

6. Marketed against the competition of:

Direct competition	Indirect competition
6.1. __________	6.1. __________
6.2. __________	6.2. __________
6.3. __________	6.3. __________

MARKET VALUE INVENTORY MATRIX

SIC #______ Industry classification ____________________

or consumer life-style ____________________

Change areas / Market values	Economic changes	Legis-lative changes	Market changes	Techno-logical changes	Compet-itive changes	Manage-ment changes	Labor force changes	Supply changes	Consum-erist changes
Business size and diversity									
Value/price relationship									
Service capability									
Distribution breadth; delivery capability									
Terms and conditions									
Technical sophistication									
Customer sensitivity									
Competitiveness									
Ethical posture									

MARKET VALUE ALIGNER

SIC #_______ Industry classification ____________________

or consumer life-style ____________________

Market values	Required strategy to align business
1. Business size and diversity	1. ____________________
2. Value/price relationship	2. ____________________
3. Service capability	3. ____________________
4. Distribution breadth and delivery capability	4. ____________________
5. Terms and conditions	5. ____________________
6. Technical sophistication	6. ____________________
7. Customer sensitivity	7. ____________________
8. Competitiveness	8. ____________________
9. Ethical posture	9. ____________________

MARKET VALUE INVENTORY MATRIX

SIC #______ Industry classification ____________________

or consumer life-style ____________________

Change areas / Market values	Economic changes	Legis- lative changes	Market changes	Techno- logical changes	Compet- itive changes	Manage- ment changes	Labor force changes	Supply changes	Consum- erist changes
Business size and diversity									
Value/price relationship									
Service capability									
Distribution breadth; delivery capability									
Terms and conditions									
Technical sophistication									
Customer sensitivity									
Competitiveness									
Ethical posture									

MARKET VALUE ALIGNER

SIC #______ Industry classification ____________________

or consumer life-style ____________________

Market values	Required strategy to align business
1. Business size and diversity	1. ____________________
2. Value/price relationship	2. ____________________
3. Service capability	3. ____________________
4. Distribution breadth and delivery capability	4. ____________________
5. Terms and conditions	5. ____________________
6. Technical sophistication	6. ____________________
7. Customer sensitivity	7. ____________________
8. Competitiveness	8. ____________________
9. Ethical posture	9. ____________________

MARKET VALUE INVENTORY MATRIX

SIC #______ Industry classification ____________________

or consumer life-style ____________________

Change areas / Market values	Economic changes	Legislative changes	Market changes	Technological changes	Competitive changes	Management changes	Labor force changes	Supply changes	Consumerist changes
Business size and diversity									
Value/price relationship									
Service capability									
Distribution breadth; delivery capability									
Terms and conditions									
Technical sophistication									
Customer sensitivity									
Competitiveness									
Ethical posture									

MARKET VALUE ALIGNER

SIC #______ Industry classification ____________________

or consumer life-style ____________________

Market values	Required strategy to align business
1. Business size and diversity	1. ____________________
2. Value/price relationship	2. ____________________
3. Service capability	3. ____________________
4. Distribution breadth and delivery capability	4. ____________________
5. Terms and conditions	5. ____________________
6. Technical sophistication	6. ____________________
7. Customer sensitivity	7. ____________________
8. Competitiveness	8. ____________________
9. Ethical posture	9. ____________________

MARKET VALUE INVENTORY MATRIX

SIC #______ Industry classification ____________________

or consumer life-style ____________________

Change areas / Market values	Economic changes	Legis-lative changes	Market changes	Techno-logical changes	Compet-itive changes	Manage-ment changes	Labor force changes	Supply changes	Consum-erist changes
Business size and diversity									
Value/price relationship									
Service capability									
Distribution breadth; delivery capability									
Terms and conditions									
Technical sophistication									
Customer sensitivity									
Competitiveness									
Ethical posture									

MARKET VALUE ALIGNER

SIC #________ Industry classification ____________________

or consumer life-style ____________________

Market values	Required strategy to align business
1. Business size and diversity	1. ____________________
2. Value/price relationship	2. ____________________
3. Service capability	3. ____________________
4. Distribution breadth and delivery capability	4. ____________________
5. Terms and conditions	5. ____________________
6. Technical sophistication	6. ____________________
7. Customer sensitivity	7. ____________________
8. Competitiveness	8. ____________________
9. Ethical posture	9. ____________________

MARKETCENTERED ORGANIZATION PLAN

SIC #________ Industry classification ________________________

or consumer life-style ________________________

MARKETCENTERED ORGANIZATION PLAN

SIC #_______ Industry classification __________________________

or consumer life-style __________________________

MARKETCENTERED ORGANIZATION PLAN

SIC #______ Industry classification ______________________

or consumer life-style ______________________

MARKETCENTERED ORGANIZATION PLAN

SIC #_______ Industry classification __________________________

or consumer life-style ___________________________

MARKETCENTERED ORGANIZATION CHART

SIC #______ Industry classification ____________________

or consumer life-style ____________________

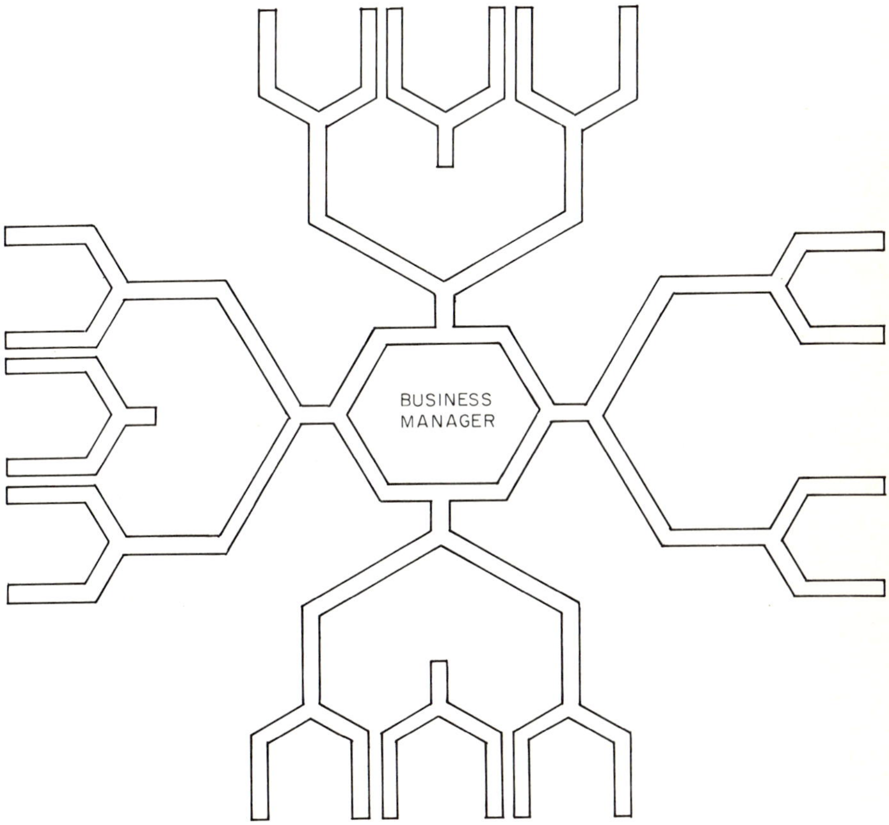

MARKETCENTERED ORGANIZATION CHART

SIC #______ Industry classification ____________________

or consumer life-style ____________________

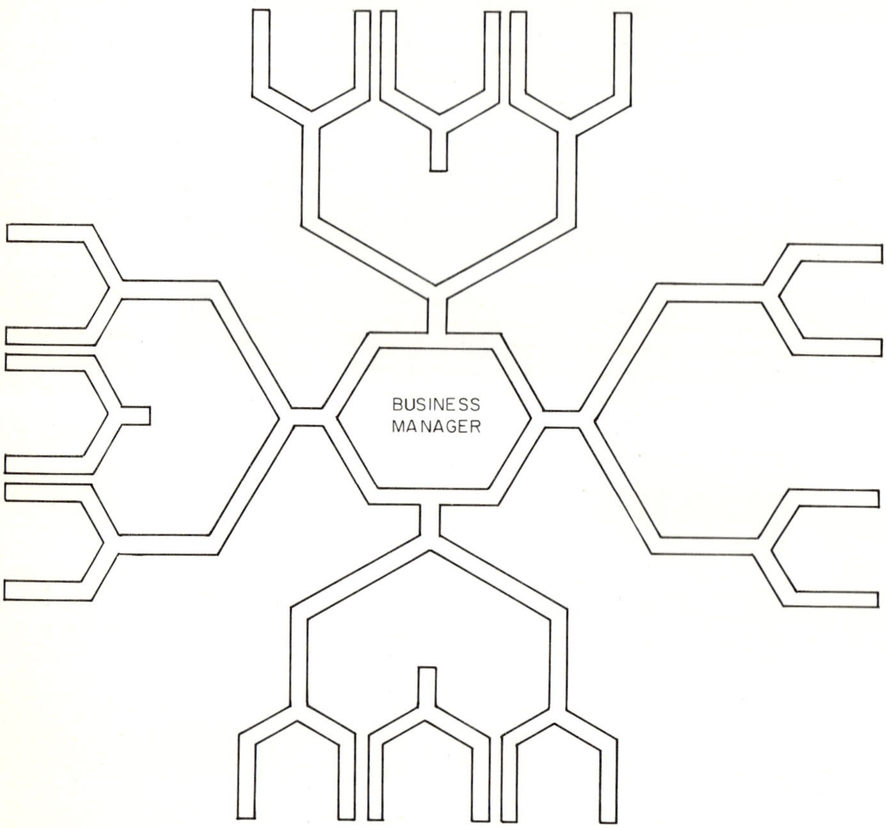

MARKETCENTERED ORGANIZATION CHART

SIC #______ Industry classification ______________________

or consumer life-style ______________________

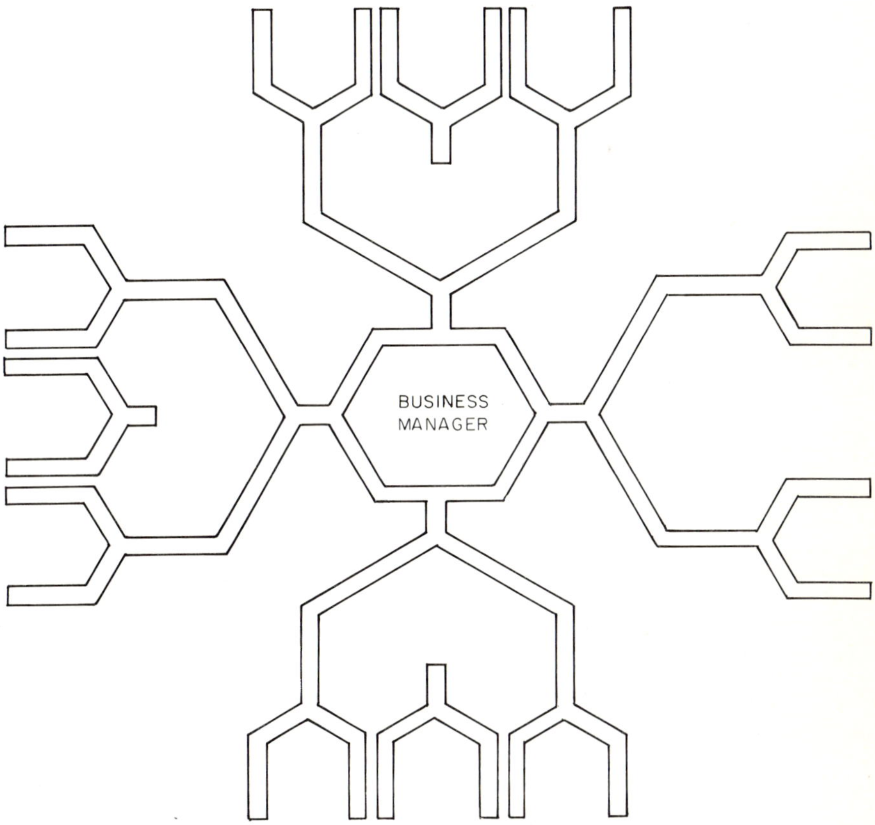

MARKETCENTERED ORGANIZATION CHART

SIC #______ Industry classification ____________________

or consumer life-style ____________________

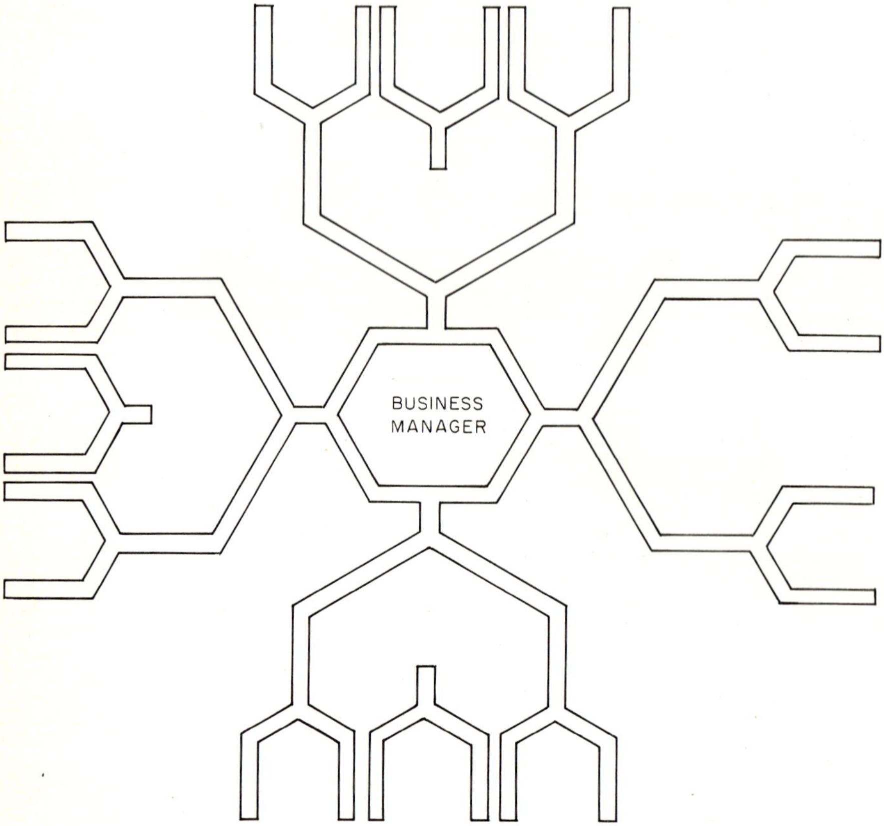

MARKETCENTERED ORGANIZATION CHART

SIC #______ Industry classification ______________________

or consumer life-style ______________________

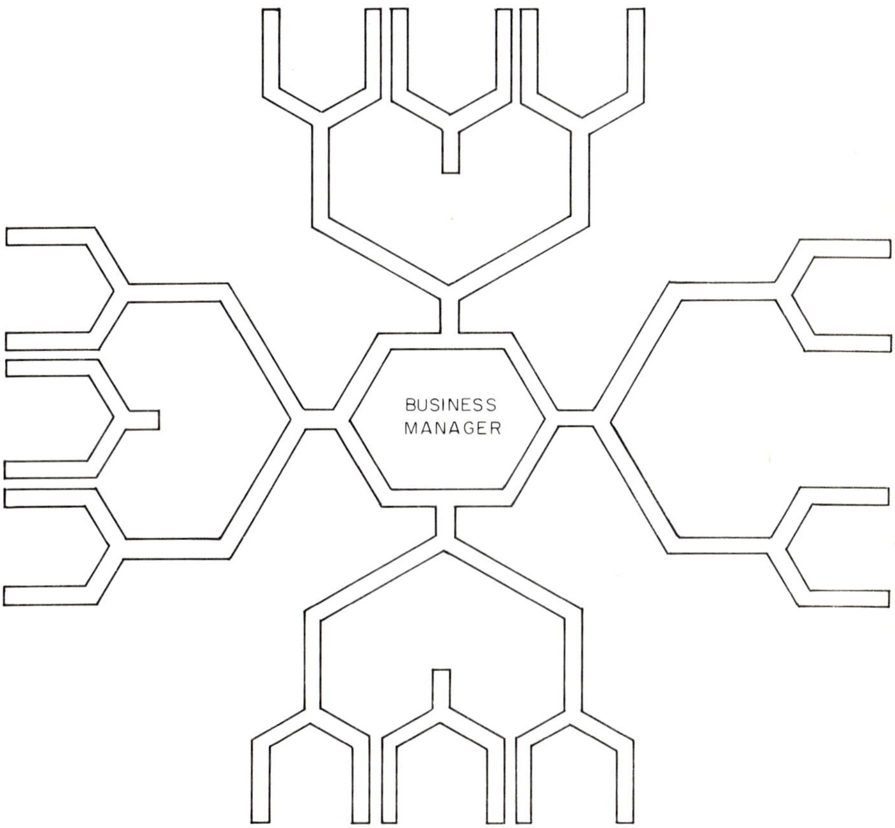

BRAND CASH FLOW/PRICING STRATEGY CORRELATION

Brand: ______________ Sold to SIC #______ Industry classification ______________

or consumer life-style ______________

	Total year (19__)	First quarter	Second quarter	Third quarter	Fourth quarter
1. At price level of:					
$__,___/unit					
Most likely cash flow will be	$___,___,___*	$__,___,___	$__,___,___	$__,___,___	$__,___,___
Best-case cash flow could be	___,___,___	__,___,___	__,___,___	__,___,___	__,___,___
Worst-case cash flow could be	___,___,___	__,___,___	__,___,___	__,___,___	__,___,___
2. At price level of:					
$__,___/unit					
Most likely cash flow will be	$___,___,___	$__,___,___	$__,___,___	$__,___,___	$__,___,___
Best-case cash flow could be	___,___,___	__,___,___	__,___,___	__,___,___	__,___,___
Worst-case cash flow could be	___,___,___	__,___,___	__,___,___	__,___,___	__,___,___

3. At price level of:

$__,___/unit

Most likely cash flow will be	$___,___,___	$__,___,___	$__,___,___	$__,___,___	$__,___,___
Best-case cash flow could be	___,___,___	__,___,___	__,___,___	__,___,___	__,___,___
Worst-case cash flow could be	___,___,___	__,___,___	__,___,___	__,___,___	__,___,___

* Common dollar value of 19__ as base year.

BRAND CASH FLOW/PRICING STRATEGY CORRELATION

Brand: ______________________ Sold to SIC #_______ Industry classification ______________________

or consumer life-style ______________________

	Total year (19__)	First quarter	Second quarter	Third quarter	Fourth quarter
1. At price level of:					
$__,___/unit					
Most likely cash flow will be	$___,___,___*	$__,___,___	$__,___,___	$__,___,___	$__,___,___
Best-case cash flow could be	___,___,___	__,___,___	__,___,___	__,___,___	__,___,___
Worst-case cash flow could be	___,___,___	__,___,___	__,___,___	__,___,___	__,___,___
2. At price level of:					
$__,___/unit					
Most likely cash flow will be	$___,___,___	$__,___,___	$__,___,___	$__,___,___	$__,___,___
Best-case cash flow could be	___,___,___	__,___,___	__,___,___	__,___,___	__,___,___
Worst-case cash flow could be	___,___,___	__,___,___	__,___,___	__,___,___	__,___,___

3. At price level of:

$__,___/unit

Most likely cash flow will be	$___,___,___	$__,___,___	$__,___,___	$__,___,___	$__,___,___
Best-case cash flow could be	___,___,___	__,___,___	__,___,___	__,___,___	__,___,___
Worst-case cash flow could be	___,___,___	__,___,___	__,___,___	__,___,___	__,___,___

* Common dollar value of 19__ as base year.

BRAND CASH FLOW/PRICING STRATEGY CORRELATION

Brand: ______________ Sold to SIC #______ Industry classification ______________

or consumer life-style ______________

	Total year (19__)	First quarter	Second quarter	Third quarter	Fourth quarter
1. At price level of:					
$__,___/unit					
Most likely cash flow will be	$___,___,___*	$__,___,___	$__,___,___	$__,___,___	$__,___,___
Best-case cash flow could be	___,___,___	__,___,___	__,___,___	__,___,___	__,___,___
Worst-case cash flow could be	___,___,___	__,___,___	__,___,___	__,___,___	__,___,___
2. At price level of:					
$__,___/unit					
Most likely cash flow will be	$___,___,___	$__,___,___	$__,___,___	$__,___,___	$__,___,___
Best-case cash flow could be	___,___,___	__,___,___	__,___,___	__,___,___	__,___,___
Worst-case cash flow could be	___,___,___	__,___,___	__,___,___	__,___,___	__,___,___

3. At price level of:

$__,___/unit

Most likely cash flow will be	$___,___,___	$__,___,___	$__,___,___	$__,___,___	$__,___,___
Best-case cash flow could be	___,___,___	__,___,___	__,___,___	__,___,___	__,___,___
Worst-case cash flow could be	___,___,___	__,___,___	__,___,___	__,___,___	__,___,___

* Common dollar value of 19__ as base year.

BRAND CASH FLOW/PRICING STRATEGY CORRELATION

Brand: ______________ Sold to SIC #______ Industry classification ______________
or consumer life-style ______________

	Total year (19__)	First quarter	Second quarter	Third quarter	Fourth quarter
1. At price level of:					
$__,___/unit					
Most likely cash flow will be	$___,___,___*	$__,___,___	$__,___,___	$__,___,___	$__,___,___
Best-case cash flow could be	___,___,___	__,___,___	__,___,___	__,___,___	__,___,___
Worst-case cash flow could be	___,___,___	__,___,___	__,___,___	__,___,___	__,___,___
2. At price level of:					
$__,___/unit					
Most likely cash flow will be	$___,___,___	$__,___,___	$__,___,___	$__,___,___	$__,___,___
Best-case cash flow could be	___,___,___	__,___,___	__,___,___	__,___,___	__,___,___
Worst-case cash flow could be	___,___,___	__,___,___	__,___,___	__,___,___	__,___,___

3. At price level of:

$__,___/unit

Most likely cash flow will be	$___,___,___	$__,___,___	$__,___,___	$__,___,___	$__,___,___
Best-case cash flow could be	___,___,___	__,___,___	__,___,___	__,___,___	__,___,___
Worst-case cash flow could be	___,___,___	__,___,___	__,___,___	__,___,___	__,___,___

* Common dollar value of 19__ as base year.

HIGH-AWARENESS ADVERTISING PLAN

Brand: ______________________________

Advertised to (heavy-profit-contributor market): SIC #______ Industry classification ________

or consumer life-style ________

1. Market need-benefit value factor

Validated market need	Single most crucial benefit to satisfy need
______________________	______________________
______________________	______________________

2. Presentation memorability factor

Style memorability	Format memorability
______________________	______________________
______________________	______________________

3. Repetitive frequency factor

Media	Frequency (times per quarter)	Market reach (#ooo)
______________________	----	---,---
______________________	----	---,---
______________________	----	---,---
______________________	----	---,---

HIGH-POSITIVE-ATTITUDE ADVERTISING PLAN

Brand: ________________________________

Advertised to (heavy-profit-contributor market): SIC #______ Industry classification ________

or consumer life-style ________

1. Superior value/price benefit positioning statement

2. Superior acquisition rationale

HIGH-AWARENESS ADVERTISING PLAN

Brand: ______________________________

Advertised to (heavy-profit-contributor market): SIC #______ Industry classification ________

or consumer life-style ________

1. Market need-benefit value factor

Validated market need	Single most crucial benefit to satisfy need
______________________	______________________
______________________	______________________

2. Presentation memorability factor

Style memorability	Format memorability
______________________	______________________
______________________	______________________

3. Repetitive frequency factor

Media	Frequency (times per quarter)	Market reach (#ooo)
______________________	----	---,---
______________________	----	---,---
______________________	----	---,---
______________________	----	---,---

HIGH-POSITIVE-ATTITUDE ADVERTISING PLAN

Brand: ____________________

Advertised to (heavy-profit-contributor market): SIC #______ Industry classification ______

or consumer life-style ______

1. Superior value/price benefit positioning statement

____

____

____

____

2. Superior acquisition rationale

____

____

____

____

HIGH-AWARENESS ADVERTISING PLAN

Brand: ______________________________

Advertised to (heavy-profit-contributor market): SIC #______ Industry classification ______

or consumer life-style ______

1. Market need-benefit value factor

Validated market need	Single most crucial benefit to satisfy need
______	______
______	______

2. Presentation memorability factor

Style memorability	Format memorability
______	______
______	______

3. Repetitive frequency factor

Media	Frequency (times per quarter)	Market reach (#ooo)
______	----	---,---
______	----	---,---
______	----	---,---
______	----	---,---

HIGH-POSITIVE-ATTITUDE ADVERTISING PLAN

Brand: ______________________________

Advertised to (heavy-profit-contributor market): SIC #______ Industry classification ________

or consumer life-style ________

1. Superior value/price benefit positioning statement

2. Superior acquisition rationale

BRANDED PRODUCT-FAMILY PROLIFERATION PLAN

Proliferable brand: ______________________

SIC #______ Industry classification ______________

or consumer life-style ______________

Single most crucial market need to be benefited	Business benefit(s) required to satisfy need	Products and services or systems required to deliver benefit(s)
______________	1. ______________	1. ______________ ______________
	2. ______________	2. ______________ ______________
	3. ______________	3. ______________ ______________
	4. ______________	4. ______________ ______________
	5. ______________	5. ______________ ______________

BRANDED PRODUCT-FAMILY PROLIFERATION PLAN

Proliferable brand: ______________________

SIC #______ Industry classification ______________

or consumer life-style ______________

Single most crucial market need to be benefited	Business benefit(s) required to satisfy need	Products and services or systems required to deliver benefit(s)
______________	1. ______________	1. ______________
	2. ______________	2. ______________
	3. ______________	3. ______________
	4. ______________	4. ______________
	5. ______________	5. ______________

BRANDED PRODUCT-FAMILY PROLIFERATION PLAN

Proliferable brand: ____________________

SIC #______ Industry classification ____________________

or consumer life-style ____________________

Single most crucial market need to be benefited	Business benefit(s) required to satisfy need	Products and services or systems required to deliver benefit(s)
____________	1. ____________	1. ____________
	2. ____________	2. ____________
	3. ____________	3. ____________
	4. ____________	4. ____________
	5. ____________	5. ____________

BRANDED PRODUCT-FAMILY PROLIFERATION PLAN

Proliferable brand: ______________________

SIC #______ Industry classification ______________________

or consumer life-style ______________________

Single most crucial market need to be benefited	Business benefit(s) required to satisfy need	Products and services or systems required to deliver benefit(s)
____________	1. ____________	1. ____________
		____________
	2. ____________	2. ____________
		____________
	3. ____________	3. ____________
		____________
	4. ____________	4. ____________
		____________
	5. ____________	5. ____________
		____________

VENTURE BUSINESS POSITIONING STATEMENT

SIC #______ Industry classification ____________________

or consumer life-style ____________________

1. Market problem to be solved and/or
market opportunity to be capitalized on by the venture

____

____

____

2. Premium benefit(s) offered by the venture
to solve market problem and/or
capitalize on market opportunity
in return for premium-pricing capability

2.1. ____________________________________

2.2. ____________________________________

2.3. ____________________________________

2.4. ____________________________________

VENTURE OBJECTIVES

SIC #______ Industry classification ______________________________

or consumer life-style ______________________________

	F19__-F19__ (Year 1)			F19__-F19__ (Year 2)			F19__-F19__ (Year 3)		
	Most likely case	Best case	Worst case	Most likely case	Best case	Worst case	Most likely case	Best case	Worst case
1. Financial objectives									
1.1. Return on investment (%)	__	__	__	__	__	__	__	__	__
1.2. Net-profit contribution after taxes ($000)	$__,___	$__,___	$__,___	$__,___	$__,___	$__,___	$__,___	$__,___	$__,___
1.3. Cash flow ($000)	$__,___	$__,___	$__,___	$__,___	$__,___	$__,___	$__,___	$__,___	$__,___
1.4. Annual earnings growth contribution based on 19__ constant dollars (%)	__	__	__	__	__	__	__	__	__
2. Sales objectives									
2.1. Sales volume (#000)	#__,___	#__,___	#__,___	#__,___	#__,___	#__,___	#__,___	#__,___	#__,___
2.2. Sales volume ($000)	$__,___	$__,___	$__,___	$__,___	$__,___	$__,___	$__,___	$__,___	$__,___
2.3. Market share (%)	__	__	__	__	__	__	__	__	__

VENTURE BUSINESS POSITIONING STATEMENT

SIC #_______ Industry classification ____________________

or consumer life-style ____________________

1. Market problem to be solved and/or
   market opportunity to be capitalized on by the venture

   ____

   ____

   ____

2. Premium benefit(s) offered by the venture
   to solve market problem and/or
   capitalize on market opportunity
   in return for premium-pricing capability

   2.1. ____________________________________

   2.2. ____________________________________

   2.3. ____________________________________

   2.4. ____________________________________

VENTURE OBJECTIVES

SIC #______ Industry classification ______________________________

or consumer life-style ______________________________

	F19__-F19__ (Year 1)			F19__-F19__ (Year 2)			F19__-F19__ (Year 3)		
	Most likely case	Best case	Worst case	Most likely case	Best case	Worst case	Most likely case	Best case	Worst case
1. Financial objectives									
1.1. Return on investment (%)	__	__	__	__	__	__	__	__	__
1.2. Net-profit contribution after taxes ($000)	$__,___	$__,___	$__,___	$__,___	$__,___	$__,___	$__,___	$__,___	$__,___
1.3. Cash flow ($000)	$__,___	$__,___	$__,___	$__,___	$__,___	$__,___	$__,___	$__,___	$__,___
1.4. Annual earnings growth contribution based on 19__ constant dollars (%)	__	__	__	__	__	__	__	__	__
2. Sales objectives									
2.1. Sales volume (#000)	#__,___	#__,___	#__,___	#__,___	#__,___	#__,___	#__,___	#__,___	#__,___
2.2. Sales volume ($000)	$__,___	$__,___	$__,___	$__,___	$__,___	$__,___	$__,___	$__,___	$__,___
2.3. Market share (%)	__	__	__	__	__	__	__	__	__

JOINT VENTURE POSITIONING STATEMENT

SIC #______ Industry classification ____________________

or consumer life-style ____________________

1. Market problem to be solved and/or
market opportunity to be capitalized on by the venture

____

____

____

2. Premium benefit(s) offered by the venture
to solve market problem and/or
capitalize on market opportunity
in return for premium-pricing capability

2.1. ____________________________________

2.2. ____________________________________

2.3. ____________________________________

2.4. ____________________________________

JOINT VENTURE OBJECTIVES

SIC #______ Industry classification ____________________

or consumer life-style ____________________

	F19__-F19__ (Year 1)			F19__-F19__ (Year 2)			F19__-F19__ (Year 3)		
	Most likely case	Best case	Worst case	Most likely case	Best case	Worst case	Most likely case	Best case	Worst case
1. Financial objectives									
1.1. Return on investment (%)	--	--	--	--	--	--	--	--	--
1.2. Net-profit contribution after taxes ($000)	$--,---	$--,---	$--,---	$--,---	$--,---	$--,---	$--,---	$--,---	$--,---
1.3. Cash flow ($000)	$--,---	$--,---	$--,---	$--,---	$--,---	$--,---	$--,---	$--,---	$--,---
1.4. Annual earnings growth contribution based on 19__ constant dollars (%)	--	--	--	--	--	--	--	--	--
2. Sales objectives									
2.1. Sales volume (#000)	#--,---	#--,---	#--,---	#--,---	#--,---	#--,---	#--,---	#--,---	#--,---
2.2. Sales volume ($000)	$--,---	$--,---	$--,---	$--,---	$--,---	$--,---	$--,---	$--,---	$--,---
2.3. Market share (%)	--	--	--	--	--	--	--	--	--

JOINT VENTURE POSITIONING STATEMENT

SIC #______ Industry classification ____________________

or consumer life-style ____________________

1. Market problem to be solved and/or
   market opportunity to be capitalized on by the venture

   ____

   ____

   ____

2. Premium benefit(s) offered by the venture
   to solve market problem and/or
   capitalize on market opportunity
   in return for premium-pricing capability

   2.1. ____________________

   2.2. ____________________

   2.3. ____________________

   2.4. ____________________

JOINT VENTURE OBJECTIVES

SIC #______ Industry classification ______________________________

or consumer life-style ______________________________

	F19__-F19__ (Year 1)			F19__-F19__ (Year 2)			F19__-F19__ (Year 3)		
	Most likely case	Best case	Worst case	Most likely case	Best case	Worst case	Most likely case	Best case	Worst case
1. Financial objectives									
1.1. Return on investment (%)	--	--	--	--	--	--	--	--	--
1.2. Net-profit contribution after taxes ($000)	$--,---	$--,---	$--,---	$--,---	$--,---	$--,---	$--,---	$--,---	$--,---
1.3. Cash flow ($000)	$--,---	$--,---	$--,---	$--,---	$--,---	$--,---	$--,---	$--,---	$--,---
1.4. Annual earnings growth contribution based on 19__ constant dollars (%)	--	--	--	--	--	--	--	--	--
2. Sales objectives									
2.1. Sales volume (#000)	#--,---	#--,---	#--,---	#--,---	#--,---	#--,---	#--,---	#--,---	#--,---
2.2. Sales volume ($000)	$--,---	$--,---	$--,---	$--,---	$--,---	$--,---	$--,---	$--,---	$--,---
2.3. Market share (%)	--	--	--	--	--	--	--	--	--

ACQUISITION BUSINESS POSITIONING STATEMENT

SIC #______ Industry classification ______________________

or consumer life-style ______________________

1. Market problem to be solved and/or
   market opportunity to be capitalized on by the venture

   ____

   ____

   ____

2. Premium benefit(s) offered by the venture
   to solve market problem and/or
   capitalize on market opportunity
   in return for premium-pricing capability

   2.1. ____

   2.2. ____

   2.3. ____

   2.4. ____

ACQUISITION OBJECTIVES

SIC #______ Industry classification ________________________________

or consumer life-style ________________________________

	F19__-F19__ (Year 1)			F19__-F19__ (Year 2)			F19__-F19__ (Year 3)		
	Most likely case	Best case	Worst case	Most likely case	Best case	Worst case	Most likely case	Best case	Worst case
1. Financial objectives									
1.1. Return on investment (%)	--	--	--	--	--	--	--	--	--
1.2. Net-profit contribution after taxes ($000)	$--,---	$--,---	$--,---	$--,---	$--,---	$--,---	$--,---	$--,---	$--,---
1.3. Cash flow ($000)	$--,---	$--,---	$--,---	$--,---	$--,---	$--,---	$--,---	$--,---	$--,---
1.4. Annual earnings growth contribution based on 19__ constant dollars (%)	--	--	--	--	--	--	--	--	--
2. Sales objectives									
2.1. Sales volume (#000)	#--,---	#--,---	#--,---	#--,---	#--,---	#--,---	#--,---	#--,---	#--,---
2.2. Sales volume ($000)	$--,---	$--,---	$--,---	$--,---	$--,---	$--,---	$--,---	$--,---	$--,---
2.3. Market share (%)	--	--	--	--	--	--	--	--	--

ACQUISITION BUSINESS POSITIONING STATEMENT

SIC #______ Industry classification ____________________

or consumer life-style ____________________

1. Market problem to be solved and/or
market opportunity to be capitalized on by the venture

____

____

____

2. Premium benefit(s) offered by the venture
to solve market problem and/or
capitalize on market opportunity
in return for premium-pricing capability

2.1. ____________________________________

2.2. ____________________________________

2.3. ____________________________________

2.4. ____________________________________

ACQUISITION OBJECTIVES

SIC #______ Industry classification ______________________________

or consumer life-style ______________________________

	F19__-F19__ (Year 1)			F19__-F19__ (Year 2)			F19__-F19__ (Year 3)		
	Most likely case	Best case	Worst case	Most likely case	Best case	Worst case	Most likely case	Best case	Worst case
1. Financial objectives									
1.1. Return on investment (%)	--	--	--	--	--	--	--	--	--
1.2. Net-profit contribution after taxes ($000)	$--,---	$--,---	$--,---	$--,---	$--,---	$--,---	$--,---	$--,---	$--,---
1.3. Cash flow ($000)	$--,---	$--,---	$--,---	$--,---	$--,---	$--,---	$--,---	$--,---	$--,---
1.4. Annual earnings growth contribution based on 19__ constant dollars (%)	--	--	--	--	--	--	--	--	--
2. Sales objectives									
2.1. Sales volume (#000)	#--,---	#--,---	#--,---	#--,---	#--,---	#--,---	#--,---	#--,---	#--,---
2.2. Sales volume ($000)	$--,---	$--,---	$--,---	$--,---	$--,---	$--,---	$--,---	$--,---	$--,---
2.3. Market share (%)	--	--	--	--	--	--	--	--	--

5

REBRANDING STRATEGY THRUSTS

There are eight growth-planning strategies for rebranding commodities:

1. Product repositioning and repricing
2. System packaging
3. System pricing
4. Market value realignment
5. Marketcentered sales organization
6. Vertical integration
7. Consultative selling
8. Profit-improvement advertising

Commodity products that have survived to maturity are often former brands. They belong in Category 4 of our four-part product classification system. Mature commodities usually have leading competitive positions in slow-growth or no-growth markets. They generally serve their markets with an established benefit that has been replicated and standardized by competition. Mature commodities are the mainstays of their product lines, sometimes contributing the greatest cash flow for capital investment purposes. Their profit per unit of sale is generally lower than brand profit, but their unit sales volume can be exceedingly high. For this reason, mature commodities are frequently the key to revenue production. When they fade, revenues fade with them.

A brand degenerates into commodity status when its market perceives that the product's value has been exceeded by its price. This can come about because competitors have neutralized the product's former benefit advantage or because the product's technology has been obsoleted by another way of delivering the same benefit or a better one. The market then sets about pressing down on price to bring it into balance with value. Either outright price concessions or added values in the form of deals, discounts, or other premiums such as free services will be demanded. By means of this type of price-centered transaction, the market is saying that since it cannot perceive any preferential value in the product, it will seek a preferential value in the product's price.

Commodity prices, like brand prices, are set by their markets. But they are set on the low side. The commodity manufacturer's objective is to maintain list price. The market's objective is to downgrade it. To hold margins, the manufacturer can only lower cost. To hold value at a point above price, the market can only keep bringing price down closer to cost. Time and competition are on the market's side. This is why a product line consisting only of mature commodities is in trouble.

The converse, however, is also true. Product lines without at least one Category 4 mature commodity can be in trouble. They lack a cash-flow machine. They probably lack broad-scale market acceptance as well, together with the established high awareness of both the product and its maker and the strong, positive attitudes that only a mature commodity can earn. While it may be bedeviled by its customers and competitors, both of whom strive to bring its margins ever closer to its cost base, a mature commodity that has achieved market leadership can be the mightiest profit maker of all. If it can be rebranded, that is, given the ability to merit higher margins based on value pricing as opposed to a commodity's typically low-margin/high-volume basis of business, significant new capital can often be generated at relatively low incremental cost.

Commodity Turnaround Screens

Two filtering approaches should be adopted before you plan to turn a mature-commodity business around. First, you should make sure that the product is a mature commodity. Second, you should make sure that it is cost-effective to try to turn it around.

A mature commodity is a product whose earnings have peaked. It may be generating considerable cash flow, but it has passed the half-life point in earnings: more than half of its earning span has ended. Demand may ebb and flow, but zero growth prevails, or, at best, growth occurs at the pace of the gross national product. This means, at best, that market growth is occurring only at the replacement rate. At worst, negative growth is slowly increasing.

As a consequence, competition is centered largely on price. Margins become depressed, and cost control is a key function. Product differences between competitors are marginal. All rival products conform to the same general specifications, making them extremely sensitive to substitution. Price concessions, deals and discounts, and free services are the principal differentiators. There is little or no technological change, or if any such change occurs, it is quickly knocked off by replication. Self-manufacture by major customers is therefore a viable alternative to purchase and may come to represent the major competitive threat to product survival.

Mature commodity businesses are run in maintenance style. Manufacturing efficiency, process cost reduction, and distribution efficiency and cost control are essential to maintaining margins. Everything that is done in a commodity business must attempt to maximize cash flow and minimize capital investment.

Questions that begin with "When" are rarely heard from customers. Instead, they ask "Why is your price so high?" and "How much lower can you go?"

If you market a consumer product, your sales strategies will center on price-off campaigns, retailer premiums, deals and discounts, and periodic advertising of "new and improved" ingredients. You will require significant volume to compensate for low margins. So will your retailers. Turnover through sales will be your strategic focal point.

If you market an industrial product, you will be doing most of your business on the 3:3 basis shown as Commodity Country in Exhibit 1-2. In Commodity Country, sales are based on price. As a result, the purchasing levels of customer decision making will be your major sales interface. Your basic sales approach will be to meet specifications at the lowest price, fortified with various concessions to add value to the deal and further discount price. In these ways, you will be involuntarily helping to improve customer profit to the detriment on your own.

Exhibits 5-1 and 5-2 are correlates of Exhibit 1-2. They show the location of Commodity Country on the classic life-cycle curve. In Exhibit 5-1, the horizontal base line represents commercial time: the number of years during which a product has been on the market. The vertical axis represents gross sales volume. At Phase A, the product is new; sales are below break-even. Profitable sales volume begins to be generated at Phase B, in which the product has entered Brand Country. Its profits tend to run ahead of its sales. Commodity Country has been reached at Phase C. The product is still adding importantly to profits, but its profit per unit is probably in a state of decline. Holding margins has become precarious.

To employ life-cycle analysis to sweep your product lines for mature-commodity products that are candidates for rebranding, use a separate copy of Planning Page 43 to locate the approximate position of every product on an individual product-line basis. Use Exhibit 5-2 as a guide. Assign the proper gross sales dollar volume and commercial-year values to each axis on the planning pages. Then plot the position of every product according to the gross dollar volume that it is contributing in the current year of its commercial life. Use triangles to represent new products, squares to represent big-winner brands, and circles to represent commodity products.

EXHIBIT 5-1

PROFIT, SALES, AND INVESTMENT OVER THE LIFE CYCLE

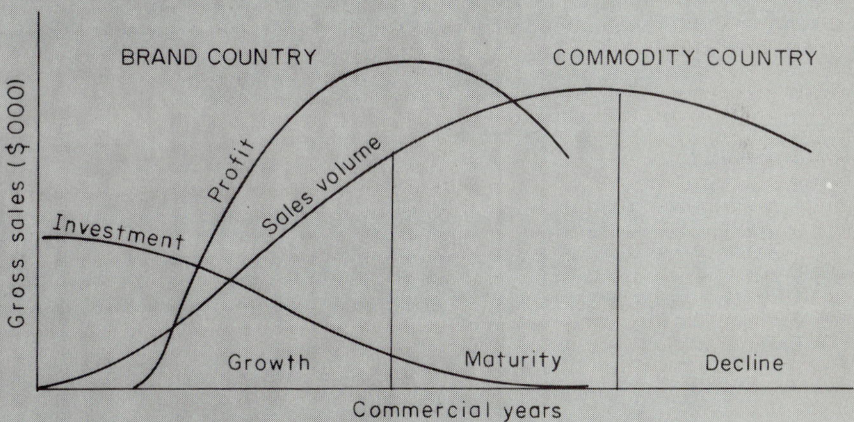

EXHIBIT 5-2

CLASSIC LIFE CYCLE

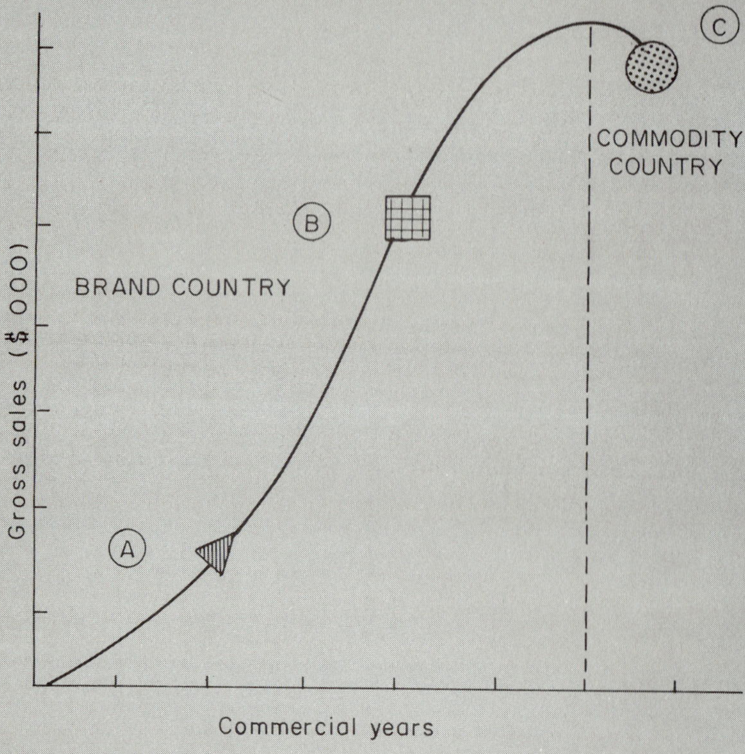

Renovation or Systems: The Critical Choice

There are two basic approaches to rebranding a commodity business. Selection of the proper approach represents a critical choice. If the wrong choice is made, the opportunity to rebrand may be irretrievably lost.

One approach is through the *marginal renovation* of a commodity product. Renovation can be achieved by either of two strategies, technical renovation plus marketing renovation or marketing renovation alone. In both options, the marketing function must undergo renovation because only marketing and not technology can transmit the perception of added user value that justifies premium price.

Marlboro cigarettes and Pontiac motor cars are examples of products that have been marginally renovated by adding marketing value. Marlboros were rebranded from their original positioning as a woman's product to a virile, ultra-macho masculine cigarette. Pontiac was rebranded by being "youthetized" from an older-folks type of car. At the same time, De Soto tried a similar repositioning but fell to its death between the cracks separating the two positions.

Arm & Hammer baking soda made its change not by switching markets but by switching uses, moving from a position as a cooking ingredient to one as a refrigerator air freshener. Jell-O has a long track record of periodically rebranding itself through new uses in order to keep justifying its premium price. Grape Nuts and Shredded Wheat have each applied the Pontiac approach to move from positions as middle-aged and senior citizens' laxatives to become somewhat more of a mass-market health aid. Frank Perdue has branded chicken, and Chiquita Banana has branded bananas. But the fact remains that most turned-around commodities have not made it on their own.

There are two basic criteria that can be used to screen in commodities for renovation planning. One criterion is the susceptibility of the commodities to the cost-effective application of marginal technical renovation. The screening questions asked here are designed to define the "technical hurdle" to rebranding:

1. What is the nature and cost of the minimal technical investment that can be added to this product's cost base so that it can command a premium price?
2. What is the most likely return that can be contributed by this investment in terms of net incremental profit?
3. Does this most likely return on investment represent an acceptable rate in terms of corporate criteria for capital commitment; that is, is it equal to or better than competitive allocations of the same resources, and is it the best allocation of technical resources that can be made at this time?

The second criterion is a commodity product's susceptibility to the cost-effective application of sales and marketing renovation. The screening questions to be asked here are designed to define the "marketing hurdle" to rebranding:

1. What is the nature and cost of the minimal sales and marketing investment that can be added to this product's cost base so that it can command a premium price?
2. What is the most likely return that can be contributed by this investment in terms of net incremental profit?
3. Does this most likely return on investment represent an acceptable rate in terms of corporate criteria for capital commitment; that is, is it equal to or better than competitive allocations of the same resources, and is it the best allocation of marketing resources that can be made at this time?

There are times when a side-by-side comparison of the net-profit increments will indicate which cut to take at rebranding a commodity, a technical cut or a marketing cut. The two approaches will frequently have to be combined, but the decision will not always be clean. Rebranding decisions may have to be made on other grounds than a product's most likely return. The product's ability to contribute to the return from allied products in its line or to contribute to the return from a comprehensive system in which it is packaged may have partial or wholly determining effects on the decision to go ahead with rebranding.

The second approach to rebranding is through embedding a commodity product in a *system* composed of related products and services. A system shelters a commodity from price sensitivity by surrounding it with value-adding products and services so that the system can solve more comprehensive market problems than any of its components alone. The key components that enable a system to be brandable are its applications consultant, who prescribes and manages it, and the information base on customer costs and sales opportunities to which the consultant has access.

Eight Strategy Thrusts

Once a renovative or systems approach has been decided on as the best way to achieve rebranding, there are eight strategy thrusts that you can mix and match to accelerate the growth of mature commodities:

1. Product repositioning and repricing
2. System packaging

3. System pricing
4. Market value realignment
5. Marketcentered sales organization
6. Vertical integration
7. Consultative selling
8. Profit-improvement advertising

Not all commodities will require all eight thrusts. The mix and match will differ almost every time. Even if the elements are no different, their allocated emphasis will be. The best rule to follow is the rule for brand building itself: tailor every growth thrust to its minimal requirements so that you can ensure cost-effective commodity rebranding.

5-1 PRODUCT REPOSITIONING AND REPRICING

Of the two basic strategies for rebranding a mature commodity product, adding marketing or technical value and packaging the product into a system, you should consider the feasibility and cost effectiveness of adding new marketing or technical value. If you elect to reposition a commodity by taking an added-value approach through marketing or technological renovation, use Planning Page 44 to reposition the product in line with a heavy-profit-contributor market's single most crucial need. Then use Planning Page 45. This page is a format for correlating cash flow and commodity-repricing strategy on a quarter-by-quarter basis. Use a separate copy of the planning page to calculate the cash flows that can most likely be generated at various price levels in every target market.

5-2 SYSTEMS PACKAGING[1]

System packaging strategy is the second option for rebranding a commodity product. A system is a comprehensive unit composed of one or more commodity products and related services. It is custom-tailored in a package to solve a comprehensive customer problem. The system's products and services work together to provide a more comprehensive benefit than any one of them could yield alone. They are marketed as a single package. Because of the single-unit nature of their marketing, systems are excellent carriers of commodity products. When a commodity is tucked inside a system, it loses its individual identity. Whereas it could never command a premium price standing alone, it can contribute significant

[1] A more detailed treatment of this subject can be found in Mack Hanan et al., *Systems Selling Strategies*, American Management Association, New York, 1977.

added value to a system and therefore to the system's ability to sell at a premium.

In commodity-product selling, the product itself is sold. Since it can add no premium value, it commands no premium price. In system selling, a profit-improvement solution to a customer problem is sold. It can add demonstrable premium value in reduced costs or increased sales revenues. It can therefore command a premium price.

Systems can be branded because of their preemptive value. This is true even though some, many, or all of the system's components are commodities. Since it is not the components that are being sold, systems are never priced at the sum of the costs of their component parts. The premium benefit of a system that justifies a premium price is its ability to improve customer profit over and above its cost. Systems are priced on a return-on-investment, not a cost-plus, basis.

The electronics industry has led the way in systems selling. Product application services, performance monitoring and upgrading services, and teaching and financing services have customarily accompanied equipment sales. Companies in many diverse industries are packaging a commodity product together with other related products or services and marketing them as an integrated package that can support a premium price.

Systems are typically composed of three types of components:

1. A salesperson's *professional expertise* in managing the prescription of the system and its application, monitoring, and upgrading.
2. One or more products, which represent the system's *hardware.*
3. One or more services, which represent the system's *software.* Services may be of two types. Product-related services such as preventive-maintenance, repair, and replacement services are one type. The other type consists of educational and information services.

A system package may contain a single unit of hardware or several pieces of equipment. It may be surrounded by one or two services or more than a dozen. In Exhibit 5-3, a comprehensive fourteen-unit service package is shown as a response to solving materials cleaning and finishing problems. The services surrounding the cleaning and finishing equipment include identification of needs for a system; prescription of a system to benefit these needs; design, operation, and maintenance of the system; financing it; repair, replacement, and resupply services; customer employee education; guidance in legislative compliance with environmental codes and in employee and community relations; access to supplier in-

EXHIBIT 5-3

MATERIALS CLEANING AND FINISHING SYSTEM

1. Customer problem-solving/needs analysis
2. System prescription
3. System design, engineering, and construction
4. System operation and maintenance
5. System financing
6. System repair, replacement, and resupply
7. System operation and maintenance education
8. System compliance with legislative codes
9. Customer process profit improvement
10. Customer process by-product marketing
11. Customer process raw-materials recycling
12. Customer guidance in merchandising system benefits through employee and community public relations
13. Customer access to research and development innovations
14. Customer access to supplier information resources on customer process improvement

formation and R&D innovations; search for cost savings and new income sources through the collection and recycling of raw materials as well as by-product marketing; and, of course, the ultimate benefit of profit improvement.

Model System Packages

A seller of office communications systems defines the business mission of office systems as improving the profit of customer work-processing functions. The communication of words back and forth in business offices is the vital customer process on which the seller's systems concentrate to solve problems of rising communications costs and inefficiencies in communication. The seller prescribes a total communication system as opposed to the random use of a typewriter here, a dictating machine there, and a copying machine somewhere else. The system is composed of input and output processing equipment and inspection, maintenance, repair, replacement, resupply, financing, and educational services.

A seller of fire protection systems defines the business mission of fire systems as improving the efficiency and reducing the cost of safeguarding customer chemical-processing functions. The refining of chemical compounds in laboratories is the vital customer process on which the seller's systems concentrate to solve the problem of rising cost for high-hazard protection. The seller prescribes a total-risk management system as opposed to the random use of a fire extinguisher here, an ax and bucket of sand there, and an off-the-shelf employee training program somewhere else. The system is composed of fire detection and extinguishing equipment and inspection, maintenance, repair, replacement, resupply, financing, and educational services. Working with these tools, the seller analyzes and defines fire protection problems from both a physical-hazard perspective and a legislative-compliance point of view. The end objective is to be able to insure customers against loss of business-income continuity due to fire.

A seller of materials cleaning systems defines the business mission of cleaning systems as improving the profit of customer electric-motor–rebuilding processes. Cleaning and repainting electric motors constitute the vital customer process on which the seller's systems concentrate to solve the problem of rising costs for removing dirt, grease, rust, and paint. The seller prescribes a total cleaning and finishing system as opposed to the random use of a sandblasting machine here, a blast room there, and steel-grit abrasives somewhere else. The system is composed of blasting equipment, consumable abrasives, and related inspection, maintenance, repair, replacement, resupply, financing, and educational services.

Responding to Customer Signals

The signal to prescribe a system comes from a customer. It generally takes the form of a problem. There are three major classes of customer problems that can be responded to successfully by prescribing a system:

1. A product is "too expensive" or "no better than competition."
2. A product requires "frequent servicing" or "sophisticated knowledge" to operate or maintain.
3. A product is subject to "rapid depreciation" or "technological obsolescence."

Systemizing Products That are "Too Expensive" or "No Better than Competition"

If your market says that one of your products is too expensive or no better than competition, it is classifying the product as a commodity rather than as a branded speciality. Commodities are utilities. Utilities are interchangeable. One supplier's utility is generally no better or no worse than competitive utilities. Since the only point of difference between utilities is the price at which they can be purchased, markets haggle with utility suppliers to drive price down as close as possible to cost.

Systemizing a commodity product can often answer the two objections of expensiveness and competitive parity. The added values offered by the system as a whole may help to justify a new, higher price. By their inclusion in the system, commodity components may be able to bring worthwhile benefits that the product alone cannot deliver. If one or more of the components offers a unique benefit, its branded nature can help maintain a premium-price umbrella over the entire system.

One of the most helpful components that can justify a branded price is the offering of a phased-payment financing plan to obtain the system. Because it spreads price out over time, a financing plan can take the onus off total price. The cost advantages of financing also act to reduce the effect of price. Up-front capital expenditure is avoided, allowing customers to use their funds for investment purposes or other purchases. Certain tax advantages may also be possible. If the financing plan is presented as a service fee for use of the system's benefits rather than as a price, it may help make the system as a whole more acceptable.

If you elect to systemize a product or a piece of equipment that has been classified by its market as too expensive, use Planning Page 46. If you elect to systemize a product or a piece of equipment whose benefits have been neutralized by competition or are perceived by customers to have been neutralized, use Planning Page 47. In either case, plan the most cost-effective system that will contain all the components you believe necessary (but only enough to be sufficient) to package it so as to justify a premium price. Then calculate the system's total cost to supply the added value it can deliver to customer operations and its total price. Added value must exceed price if the system is to be marketable. Price must exceed cost if the system is to be profitable. Use a separate copy of the planning page for every such system you want to sell to every market segment.

Systemizing Products That Are Subject to Rapid Depreciation or Technological Obsolescence

If one of your products is subject to rapid depreciation, its market may have relegated it to commodity status because the product can make only a short-term contribution to value. It may simply not be worth getting excited about. Products whose technology can become rapidly obsolete share a similar burden. In addition, they may also find it difficult to justify a premium price.

Systemizing a product that is subject to relatively rapid depreciation or technical obsolescence can often protect it from price erosion. The system's added values help take customer attention away from concentrating on the product. Even though the product may originally have been technologically unique, marketing strategy should not be nostalgic. It should focus on the preemptive value of the present system. This will provide a market positioning for the system that may be enforceable over something longer than the short term. Otherwise, premium-price opportunity will be lost as soon as the product is knocked down to scientific equality by a competitor.

A vital component of most systems designed to counter a product's depreciation or technical obsolescence is some form of leasing basis for obtaining the system. If the system can be paid for over time, some of the curse is taken off depreciation and obsolescence since customers are no longer required to commit themselves to a front-end price that forms a dramatic background for continuing loss of value. The money saved can be invested at a return or used for other purchases. In this way, a lease can endow both a commodity-based system and the customer's capital funds with added value.

A second benefit of including a lease option in a system for a rapidly depreciating or obsoleting product is that provision can be made within the lease for periodic replacement or upgrading. These services defray the costs of obsolescence by maintaining the system in a state of modernity at all times. When a lease provides this service, it can be marketed as a service-fee method of maintaining a system's original value.

If you elect to systemize a commodity product or piece of equipment that is subject to rapid depreciation after purchase, use Planning Page 48. If you elect to systemize a commodity product or piece of equipment that may be subject to accelerated technological obsolescence, use Planning Page 49. In either case, plan the most cost-effective system that will contain all the components you believe necessary (but only enough to be sufficient) to package it so as to justify a premium price. Then calculate the system's total cost to supply the added value it can deliver to customer operations and its total price. Added value must exceed price if the system is to be marketable. Price must exceed cost if the system is to be profitable. Use a separate copy of the planning page for every such system you want to sell to every market segment.

Systemizing Products That Require Frequent Servicing or Sophisticated Knowledge

If one of your product's normal-use situations requires predictable periodic servicing, replacement parts or reordered consumables, or sophisticated knowledge, it is a natural candidate for systemizing. In this type of situation, the classic systems strategy of the "razor and the blades" can come into play. The product or equipment can act as the razor. It is a one-time or long-term sale. The servicing it requires or its replacement parts and consumables can act as the blades that must be reordered through repeat sales. Over the service life of the product, sales of the blades will account for the major source of the system's contribution to profit.

The blades can also provide a second benefit. They give a salesperson a valid, profit-making reason to return again and again to monitor the system's performance within the customer's process. This offers the opportunity to seek new or further needs to supply, to maintain the system's performance so that is operates in the most cost-effective manner for the customer, and to upgrade the system whenever possible with more sophisticated hardware and accessories.

A razor-and-blades system may include one, two, three, or all four of the following components:

1. A periodic service agreement to provide recurrent maintenance, repair, and replacement parts and consumables.

2. An educational service to teach the customer's personnel how to operate the system. This service may involve an intensive initial teaching program supplemented by periodic refresher courses in seminar or correspondence form, printed and audio-visual instructional materials, or the conduct of a school.

3. A turnkey type of personnel service that provides work forces who are professionally trained to operate customer systems on a cost-plus-fee basis on the customer's premises. A complete staff can be provided, along with the management of its recruitment, compensation, motivation, and benefits.

4. Any or all of these three components may be provided for in a service-fee type of lease.

If you elect to systemize a commodity product or piece of equipment that requires periodic servicing, replacement parts, or consumables, use Planning Page 50. If you elect to systemize a commodity product or piece of equipment that requires a high degree of customer education for its use, use Planning Page 51. In either case, plan the most cost-effective system that will contain all the components you believe necessary (but only enough to be sufficient) to package it so as to justify a premium price. Then calculate the system's total cost to supply the added value it can deliver to customer operations and its total price. Added value must exceed price if the system is to be marketable. Price must exceed cost if the system is to be profitable. Use a separate copy of the planning page for every such system you want to sell to every market segment.

5-3 SYSTEM PRICING

From a supplier's point of view, a system's price must be a premium price because of the added costs incurred in prescribing, installing, monitoring, and maintaining systems. From the customer's point of view, a system's price can afford to be a premium because, like brand pricing, it is based on a system's ability to add a premium value. System prices should be set as high as the customer's perception of conferred value will bear. In other words, system pricing should be return-on-investment pricing.

The price of a system should be a direct correlate of the user's most likely rate of return on the system's investment. The higher the value of the return, the higher the price can be. Because system pricing is ROI pricing, there is no such thing as a fixed or list system price. For many companies, a wide range of prices will be attached to the same system. The price that applies to any given sale will be the highest price that the system's return can justify on a cost/benefit basis. In the same way that a brand can be a bargain no matter how high its price may be, it is possible for a system to be a bargain as long as cost/benefit analysis confirms that the benefit of its rate of return is greater than its cost.

System pricing at premium levels helps confer branding on a system. Premium prices can operate in a brand-building manner even if one or more commodities are component parts of a system. The marketable price of a system is product-independent; it depends only on returned value. This allows price to be greater than the sum of the costs or prices of the system's component commodities.

Return-on-investment Pricing Strategy

To price systems in a premium manner, the seller must provide customers with a demonstrable financial justification to possess a system. This financial justification must quantify the dollar costs that the customer can save and the additional profits that the customer can earn. By selling the system's profit improvement instead of its components, the seller provides a customer's decision makers with the rationale they need to endorse the system's required investment. Price then appears to be a function of return on investment, not a cost.

The profit-improvement approach to pricing provides a means of valuing the benefit of a system's use in specific dollar amounts of incremental profit. It relates the profit-improvement benefits that the customer can anticipate to the investment required to obtain them, including the price or rental fee for the system as *return on investment.*

Return on investment is a measuring rod for evaluating the improved profit contribution that a system can make to a customer. In terms of return on investment, a customer's improved profit can be defined as the ratio of *added income earned* to the amount of *added capital invested* in obtaining the system that produces it.

The return-on-investment basis for pricing relates price to a system's effects on the major operating and financial ingredients of profit making. Rather than base price on cost, the ROI approach connects price to the ways in which customer profit is actually made:

1. Profit per unit of sale in dollars
2. Turnover of operating funds
3. Funds required to finance the operations and processes of a customer's business
4. Total investment of capital employed, which includes a customer's working assets, plant, and facilities

According to the return-on-investment approach to determining price, the reason that a customer invests in a profit-improvement system is to earn a superior rate of return on the funds invested in it. This puts two kinds of pressure on a seller's profit-improvement proposals: (1) they must maximize the customer's added income, or (2) they must reduce the customer's costs.

System Financing

Premium pricing is the system seller's greatest blessing. To some customers, however, it may appear to be a curse. In such cases, the seller has two strategies to help take the curse off premium price. The basic strategy is always to emphasize a system's contribution to profit improvement. This directs customer attention to the benefits achievable from a system instead of the price that must be paid to receive them. The other strategy is to help the customer obtain a system's benefits by financing its acquisition.

There are three basic methods of system financing. One method is *cash-flow financing*. Under this method, the seller prepares a purchase plan whose terms help the customer optimize cash flow for maximum profit improvement. For example, the customer's payments can be related to different forms of depreciation so that the system's equipment can help pay for itself. A pay-as-you-depreciate schedule allows payments to decrease over a lengthy time frame as accelerated depreciation falls and maintenance costs rise. The purchase plan can be geared to a customer's business-income cycle or seasonal cycle. In either case, a deferred or skip payment schedule can permit smaller payments or even no payments at all during low-income periods.

A second method of system financing is to allow the customer to install and operate a system under a *monthly service fee* that is payable until the system's cost is paid in full. A third method of system financing is to allow the customer to *lease* a system on a perpetual rental basis.

While these last two methods differ, they share three similarities. Both methods permit a customer to obtain a system's benefits immediately, without the delay of having to wait until they can be afforded. Both substitute a series of relatively small bites of expenditure for a less easily digestible big lump, and both allow the option of purchase at any time.

Service-Fee Financing

A service-fee method of system financing lets a customer receive the service benefits of a system without the need to own the system. This is why a financing fee is called a service fee. As installments of service are received, installments of payments are made.

A service fee removes the burden of front-end–loading the cost of a system. The system is, in effect, leased to the customer until the final payment. At that time, full title passes. Making the payments periodic and thereby making the sale conditional often help the customer to desire to acquire the system. The essential appeal of this method is that it enables a major expenditure to be postponed but nonetheless provides immediate service benefits. In short, it allows the customer to have cake and eat it too.

There are two additional advantages to the service-fee method. The service fee is a time-payment, or deferred-payment, sale. It extends payment over time. It therefore offers the customer a hedge against inflation. A second advantage of extending payment over time is the probability that the seller's company will upgrade the system's performance during the life of the service fee. If this occurs, the customer can benefit by taking advantage of new technical developments as they occur at no additional cost.

Leasing

Like service-fee financing, leasing is an alternative to outright purchase. Whereas service-fee financing is a form of installment buying, leasing is a form of rental. Under a lease, a customer avoids the lump-sum cost of outright purchase. Instead, a system is rented. The customer acquires the system's benefits without owning it. In addition to receiving the benefits of the system, the customer gains by conserving cash and borrowing power.

Leasing can be the preferred option for financing a system under a wide range of conditions. Some of these conditions, such as the newness of the system's technology, its requirements for service, or the significance of its initial cost or price premium, directly depend on the system. Other conditions depend on the size and growth stage of the customer's operations to be affected by a system, the customer's previous systems experience, needs for continuity of service responsibility, and credit posture. A third set of conditions affecting leasing is determined by the selling situation. The most important of these situational factors are the economic cycle, inflationary pressures, legislative trends, and the policies and practices of competitive systems suppliers.

Essentially, leasing can be an attractive alternative to purchase whenever a system's total dollar cost appears high but the profit on freed capital can outweigh the costs or whenever asset ownership is not seen as an advantage. Some specific conditions under which leasing can be the preferred option for systems financing can be summarized as follows:

Aspects of the System

1. The system's technology is new and therefore unproven, making a high need for service probable.
2. The system's technology is subject to rapid obsolescence, either because it is new and will involve intensive innovation or because it is old and must be significantly improved.
3. The system requires a high service component.
4. The system carries a high initial cost.
5. The system's price premium is significant and must be offset as much as possible by interest savings and other financial benefits from leasing.

Aspects of the Customer

1. The customer is a small or medium-size company whose cash is limited but whose cash flow is predictable.
2. The customer is experiencing rapid growth and needs to conserve capital.
3. The customer's process to be systemized is new, and system application is therefore more than normally unpredictable.
4. The customer has experienced a failure with a competitive system's installation and is gun-shy.
5. The customer wants an unusually high degree and continuity of supplier responsibility.
6. The customer is fully borrowed to the credit limit.
7. The customer wants to keep borrowing power unimpaired.
8. The customer does not want to affect the balance sheet negatively by borrowing.

Premium-Price Justification Strategy

The system seller must aggressively promote a system's premium value of profit improvement as the validation of its price. Unselling price is not the problem. Selling profit improvement is the nature of the task.

By raising an umbrella of premium price over a system, the seller requires customers to focus their decision making on value. Instead of being defensive about price, the seller must use price to alert customers to expect unusual value. Price acts as a conditioner. It conditions the seller to overcome price dread and encourages the positioning of systems aggressively around their added values instead of apologetically around added costs.

To use price as a conditioner of the expectation of premium value, the seller must reverse the usual defensive presentation of price that says, "My system is high-priced, but it delivers premium value." Instead, price should be presented as follows: "My system carries a premium price. Therefore you can expect premium value from it." In this way, price loses its liability. It becomes the reason why added value is obtainable as well as the proof that added value is imbedded in the system.

By offering significant added value, the system seller can escape the need to be the lowest-price supplier or even a parity pricer. If the value of a system's profit-improvement benefit can be positioned at a premium level, the opportunity is created for premium pricing. Only when the premium-value/premium-price relationship is mismanaged will the system seller encounter customer objections to a system's price.

The system seller runs the risk of being accused of overpricing under one or more of the following three circumstances:

1. A customer's needs are incorrectly perceived, and so the seller prescribes the "wrong" system to benefit them. Any price is too high a price for the wrong system.
2. A system is overengineered either because customer needs have been incorrectly perceived or the seller has become distracted from the mission to provide the best benefits and instead provides the greatest number of components. In either of these situations, the system will lack the value of custom tailoring. This will make its value/price relationship too low and its price correspondingly too high.
3. A customer's perceptions are not made appreciative of the premium value of the seller's prescriptive and applications expertise and information base. The system will then be evaluated on the basis of the comparative price of its components. The price may be called too high when it is actually the customer's perceived value that is too low.

Planning Page 52 shows a format for correlating cash flow, system pricing strategy, and system return on investment on a key-account, customer-by-customer basis. Use as many copies of the planning page as you require to calculate the cash flow that can most likely be generated at various price levels with every key customer.

5-4 MARKET VALUE REALIGNMENT

Growing a rebranded commodity product or a commodity-based system at an accelerated rate requires a 1:1 alignment of business values with the values of its heavy-profit-contributor market. Planning Page 53 is a matrix that enables you to make an inventory of the current values with which you must align in your target markets. Use a separate copy of the planning page to describe the effects on every target market that every change area across the top of the matrix can have on the market value categories shown in the vertical column. (You have already made assumptions in Section 2-3 of Chapter 2 about the impact you anticipate from the change areas shown on the matrix.) Then use a separate copy of Planning Page 54 to summarize the responsive actions you must take in every target market to align your growth thrusts with the values that can encourage acceleration.

5-5 MARKETCENTERED SALES ORGANIZATION

The target market for a commodity-rebranding thrust must be centered on by a specialized, industry-dedicated sales force. The sales force should sell exclusively to the market's heavy profit contributors, to that market alone, and to no others. Salespersons will have to be taught to perceive every target account's needs for improved profit so that, as true partners of customer management, they can prescribe, install, maintain and service, monitor, and upgrade the product systems they sell.

Marketcentering a rebranded-commodity sales force brings two significant advantages. First, it is the only way to inject into a sales force an acute sensitivity to customer needs for reduced costs or for increased sales revenues. Second, it is the best way to make sure that the sales force sells complete systems to every customer by gaining the in-depth knowledge and support that can come only from dealing with a wide range of customer decision makers and their influencers.

When a sales organization is marketcentered on an industry basis, a heavy-profit-contributor market becomes the focal point of sales, distribution, and advertising for one or more product lines and their related services. The objective of the sales marketcenter is to become its market's preferred center for fulfilling needs of cost reduction and increased sales. This permits the market to be served by the sales center with packages of diversified systems containing commodity products. Alone, each commodity product would be exposed to price bidding. When the products are packaged in a system, however, premium price capability can dominate commodity price limitations.

Rebranded-commodity selling is not product or territorial selling. It is key-industry selling and, within each industry, key-account selling. The type of sales force that sells in a marketcentered manner is known by the market it serves. It derives its identity from the market. Its systems, sales tools, and sales support services are specifically *dedicated* to the market's needs. Its position descriptions are written with specific reference to the profit-improvement service it renders to the market, and very often its position titles such as market sales representative, systems consultant, or customer account representative are directly identified with their market.

The NCR Model

The sales force of NCR Corporation (formerly National Cash Register Company) sells two high-technology electronic systems that contain commodity products as their core. The systems are point-of-sale terminals for stores and electronic funds-transfer systems to link retailers and banks. Three heavy-profit-contributor markets called "vocations" have been centered on: retail, including department stores, discount and specialty stores, supermarkets and drug stores, and fast-food outlets; financial, including commercial banks and savings and loan associations; and a compendium marketcenter that includes commercial, industrial, medical, education, and government vocations. A separate sales force composed of "account specialists" is dedicated to every vocation. Systems are sold and serviced by teams that are centered on individual key accounts.

The NCR marketcentered sales organization enables each individual account specialist to sell coordinated systems of recording and sorting products to meet the market's needs. Previously, NCR sales representatives could sell only their own product lines. Since many products were commodities, price pressure was severe. Decision makers in customer companies typically were involved in dealing with several NCR representatives, no one of whom could know the sum total of the customer's numerical-control needs, let along serve them. Since the added-value contribution of NCR products was perceived, at best, as equal to competitive products, selling cost was high in relation to return, and an enduring premium-pricing capability was impossible to achieve.

Under a marketcentered form of sales organization, the same retail-industry–centered representative who sells an NCR cash-control system to a department store can also search out and serve the store's needs for NCR accounting systems and data processing systems. If a representative needs help, team support services are on the bench.

Every vocational market's full range of recording and sorting needs is becoming better known to NCR. In turn, by specializing in seeking out and serving these needs on a market-by-market basis, every one of NCR's vocation-centered sales organizations can become known for expertise in its market, almost as if it were an independent specialist company. This meets the market need in many of NCR's customer industries to deal with a specialist. It is an important market value to align with.

Market Fact Base

A marketcentered sales organization is centered organizationally on a heavy-profit-contributor market. Operationally, it is centered on an information base that stores two types of information about every centered market:

1. Where do the market's costs tend to cluster? In what processes, functions, operations, formulations, fabrications, and conversions do costs bunch up?

2. Why will the market's customers tend to buy more? What benefits, advantages, added values, and incentives will motivate a customer's customers to increase purchases?

These two fact bases are the true focal points of every marketcentered sales function because, from a commodity-selling point of view, the fact bases *are* the market. They form the foundation on which sales will be able to grow.

Use a separate copy of Planning Page 55 to plan the centering of a sales force on one or more of the key industries you serve. Refer to Section 5-2 for help in prescribing the systems to be sold by every marketcenter.

5-6 VERTICAL INTEGRATION

Once a commodity-rebranding thrust has been planned, two major constraints may inhibit it. One is a slowdown or a threat of cutoff in the supply of key raw-material ingredients and components on which the product depends. The other is a gross lack of end-user market knowledge and marketing skills. This is especially likely if you have been selling a commodity product "indirectly" to end users through middlemen: converters, formulators, and fabricators or other intermediaries.

If you fear a materials pinch, you may want to consider backward vertical integration. Acquiring a captive supply capability can diminish the impact on your rebranding thrust of slowdowns, shutoffs, or price escalations. In place of the uncertainties of buying, you can often achieve cost-saving economies and worry-saving certainties from "making" instead of buying.

If you are sensitive to a lack of end-user knowledge that can impede taking a commodity product to market in a rebranded manner, you may want to acquire the applications experience and knowledge of a forward or downstream supplier. This can give you a customer's ability to add value to an end-user market.

Both the backward and the forward forms of vertical integration can offer similar benefits. Some costs may be lowered. When a supply capability comes under ownership, cost controls may be used to lower production expenses. Since the costs of transferring materials from one division to another are almost always lower than open-market prices, purchasing economies may be obtained. So may greater certainty of supply as well as enhanced management comfort—an intangible, to be sure, but one with great and often overriding value.

When forward integration takes place, the resulting improvement in market sensitivity can increase the contribution from the new-product development, sales, and marketing functions. If a customer is captured, your selling costs may also be significantly reduced by sales force consolidation. Production schedules can be more closely integrated, and as a result additional cost advantages may accrue.

If you elect to plan a backward integration toward the acquisition of a source of supply, use a separate copy of Planning Page 56 for every market segment it will serve. Backward integrations offer you two basic choices: (1) you can acquire an existing supplier, or (2) you can install a supplier's technology without buying the business. If you elect to plan a forward integration toward the acquisition of an end user's marketing capability, use a separate copy of Planning Page 57 for every market segment it will serve. Forward integration offers you several choices. You can acquire an existing customer, dealer, or distributor, or you can acquire a contract manufacturer and combine his capability with the distribution capability of a manufacturer's representative, broker, or other sales agent.

5-7 CONSULTATIVE SELLING[2]

The consultative approach to selling affects the way a commodity product or a commodity-based system is sold, emphasizing sales force applications expertise. It also alters the nature of the product benefit, translating it from product performance to profit improvement for the customer. Improved profit can be proposed through cost reductions that the salesperson's proposals can achieve or by increased sales revenues that the salesperson can help the customer earn. The advantages of selling profit improvement rather than product performance are twofold. This method makes cost justification more acceptable, especially if premium price is involved. It does this by redefining price from being a cost to representing an investment on which a greater return can be demonstrated. Furthermore, the sale of improved profitability helps assure the repositioning of a supplier company as a service business—in this case, a business of the financial consultation service type.

The key agent in selling by consultation on customer profit improvement is a sales force that can prescribe the most cost-effective product and service system for every customer, manage its sale and installation, teach customer people how to use and maintain it, be consulted on its upgrading and eventual replacement, and document its profit-improvement benefits.

To reposition members of your sales force in a consultative mode, you must educate them to consult with every key customer account according to their answers to these two "consultative" questions:

1. How does my customer company contribute to its profit through the products and services that I sell?

[2] A more detailed treatment of this subject can be found in Mack Hanan et al., *Consultative Selling*, AMACOM, American Management Association, New York, 1973.

2. How can I help improve the contribution my products and services make to customer profit by:

   a. Learning where costs cluster in the customer operations I can affect so that I can apply my products and services to reduce them?

   b. Learning why my customer's customers buy so that I can apply my products and services to improve my customer's sales revenues?

Reducing customer costs and helping increase customer sales revenues are the only two ways to help improve customer profit. To cut costs, a sales force must know *where* they tend to accumulate. They can cluster in a customer's purchasing function, production, administration, or financial processes. Savings can come from reducing energy costs, decreasing the cost of maintenance, repair, and replacement parts, increasing the mean time between overhauls, providing on-hand or close-at-hand resupply sources, increasing product yield and equipment life, and decreasing personnel training or skill requirements. This is a representative, not an exhaustive, list. Exhibit 5-4 shows some typical profit-improvement options for cutting cost clusters. To increase sales revenues, a sales force must know *why* a customer's customers buy. Exhibit 5-5 shows some typical profit-improvement options for raising sales.

Consultative selling enables a sales force to multiply its profit contribution on sales because it permits a breakout from what Exhibit 1-2 refers to as the Level 3:3 selling interface. This is where salesmen of commodity products and customer purchasing agents are locked together in the unending war over price. By extending the range of knowledge to include, first, the customer's needs and, second, the customer's customers' needs, the sales representative can consult at Levels 1 and 2 of his heavy-profit-contributing accounts. At these levels, knowledge of where customer costs cluster and why the customer's customers buy can provide an entrée to decision-makers who will buy proprietary solutions to cost and sales problems at premium prices even though these solutions contain commodity products.

The consultative selling strategy works best when it is dedicated on an industry basis. All members of the sales force who sell to an industry can then become expert in knowing the answers to the consultative questions on industry cost clusters and customer buying motives, preferences, and trends.

Exhibit 5-6 shows a profit-improvement proposal outline that can be used as a consultative presentation tool. Exhibit 5-7 shows a costs/benefits analysis that can be used in the proposal to interpret selling price as a rate of return on investment.

EXHIBIT 5-4

PROFIT-IMPROVEMENT OPPORTUNITIES FROM CUTTING CUSTOMER COST CLUSTERS

1. From cutting customer's purchase costs

1.1. Reduce the number of types of articles in stock.
1.2. Standardize preferred items.
1.3. Shop the market for optimal supplier quality, delivery, and cost.
1.4. Centralize negotiations for major items.
1.5. Plan ahead to reduce rush procurement.
1.6. Subject bids and contracts to periodic review.
1.7. Conduct make-or-buy studies.
1.8. Speed up invoice processing to avoid discount losses.
1.9. Inspect incoming shipments to minimize damage from defects.
1.10. Speed up disposal of slow-moving inventories.
1.11. Establish most economical production or ordering quantities.
1.12. Shift burden of carrying inventories to suppliers.

2. From cutting customer's production costs

2.1. Reduce the number of operations.
2.2. Reduce the cost of one or more operations.
2.3. Combine two or more operations.
2.4. Automate operations.
2.5. Reduce labor.
2.6. Improve production scheduling.
2.7. Reduce operating time to speed up production.
2.8. Reduce insurance costs.
2.9. Reduce materials consumption.
2.10. Recycle materials.
2.11. Substitute less expensive materials or otherwise reformulate product
2.12. Reduce raw-materials inventory.
2.13. Reduce parts inventory.
2.14. Improve controls.
2.15. Simplify product and package design.
2.16. Dedicate an entire production line to one product or customer.

3. From cutting customer's production downtime

3.1. Standardize preferred items.
3.2. Shop the market for optimal supplier quality, delivery, and cost.

3.3. Plan ahead to reduce rush procurement.
3.4. Improve plant delivery system.
3.5. Inspect incoming shipments to minimize damage from defects.
3.6. Install preventive-maintenance program.
3.7. Improve personnel training.
3.8. Improve process analysis.
3.9. Establish most economical production or ordering points.
3.10. Correlate forecasting data between marketing and production.

4. From cutting customer's freight costs

4.1. Centralize negotiations for freight haulage.
4.2. Plan ahead to reduce rush procurement.
4.3. Prescribe preferred routing.
4.4. Stage incoming shipments to reduce overtime.
4.5. Reduce intraplant inventory transfers.
4.6. Utilize trucks more efficiently or buy trucks instead of renting them.
4.7. Relocate warehouses.
4.8. Reformulate product or packaging to lighten shipping weights.
4.9. Reduce handling costs.
4.10. Reduce insurance costs.

5. From cutting customer's administrative overhead

5.1. Reduce the number of types of articles in stock.
5.2. Standardize preferred items.
5.3. Plan ahead to reduce rush procurement.
5.4. Combine related items on purchase orders.
5.5. Establish most economical production or ordering points.
5.6. Shift burden of carrying inventories to suppliers.
5.7. Control additions of new articles to stock.
5.8. Take inventory cycle counts when stocks are low.
5.9. Combine two or more operations.
5.10. Decrease labor force.

6. From cutting cost of customer's working capital

6.1. Reduce the number of types of articles in stock.
6.2. Shop the market for optimal supplier quality, delivery, and cost.
6.3. Speed up disposal of slow-moving inventories.
6.4. Establish most economical production or ordering points.
6.5. Shift burden of carrying inventories to supplier.
6.6. Control additions of new articles to stock.
6.7. Correlate forecasting data between marketing and production.
6.8. Make secured short-term loans of excess cash.
6.9. Use large-supplier's credit department to obtain optimal bank interest rates.
6.10. Speed up production.
6.11. Increase process efficiency to decrease scrap and damaged or unacceptable work.
6.12. Combine two or more operations.

EXHIBIT 5-5

PROFIT-IMPROVEMENT OPPORTUNITIES FROM INCREASING CUSTOMER SALES REVENUES

1. Improve effectiveness of sales department.
2. Introduce new sizes, shapes, or materials or new and improved products.
3. Improve quality control to reduce call-backs and returns.
4. Apply creative sales promotion strategies.
5. Speed up production and distribution.
6. Reduce or eliminate unprofitable products, customers, warehouses, or territories.
7. Improve market-position image.
8. Add brand-name value.
9. Add customer benefits.
10. Extend product life.
11. Expand into new markets.
12. Increase distribution.

EXHIBIT 5-6

PROFIT-IMPROVEMENT PROPOSAL OUTLINE

1. Position a profit-impairing problem caused by:

   1.1 A reducible cluster of costs in a customer process, operation, or function.

   1.2 An unrealized customer opportunity to earn new sales revenues.

2. Prescribe the solution in terms of improved profit.

3. Prove the solution will work by describing the benefits of a system of products, services, and professional expertise that will be applied to their installation and implementation. Price the solution expressed as a positive rate of return on the customer's investment so that value is perceived as exceeding price.

4. Partner the customer by establishing common objectives through helping to monitor the solution's performance, teaching customer people cost-effective operation and maintenance practices, and renovating and renewing the solution over time.

EXHIBIT 5-7

COSTS/BENEFITS ANALYSIS
(Round all numbers to hundreds or thousands)

Incremental investment

1. Cost of proposed equipment	$______
2. Plus: Installation costs	______
3. Plus: Investment in other assets required	______
4. Minus: Avoidable costs (repairs and remodeling)	______
5. Minus: Net cash proceeds after tax adjustment for sale of properties retired as result of investment	______
6. Minus: Investment credit if applicable	______
7. Total cost (sum of 1–6)	______

Cost/benefit (annual basis)

	A *Present or competitive*	*B* *Your proposal*
8. Sales revenue	$______	$______
9. Minus: Variable costs:		
10. Labor (including fringe benefits)	______	______
11. Materials	______	______
12. Maintenance	______	______

	A *Present or competitive*	B *Your proposal*
13. Other variable costs	________	________
14. Total variable costs (10–13)	________	________
15. Contribution margin (8–14)	________	________
16. Minus: Fixed costs:		
17. Rent or depreciation on equipment	________	________
18. Other fixed costs	________	________
19. Total fixed costs (17 and 18)	________	________
20. Net income before taxes (15–19)	________	________
21. Proposal advantage		________

Accounting rate of return on proposed investment

22. Total investment cost (Line 7) $________

23. Average net income before taxes (Line 20) $________

24. Before tax rate of return (Line 23 ÷ Line 22) ______%

5-8 PROFIT-IMPROVEMENT ADVERTISING

In rebranding a commodity product or branding a commodity-based system, the role of advertising is to focus a target market's awareness on the ability of the product's system to improve customer profit. Commodity-rebranding advertising is customer profit-improvement advertising.

Rebranding advertising strategy must avoid debate on the merits of one system against another. Component comparisons, performance comparisons, or even system comparisons in which hardware becomes the leading edge of what is being advertised are all negative influences that can reduce system selling to simply a higher-cost form of commodity selling.

Rebranded commodity systems must emulate brand approaches in one major sense: they must talk benefits, not features, and the benefit of a system is always to be found in its ability to improve the user's profit. The economic reward of a system is what should be advertised for sale since that is what will inevitably be bought.

Rebranded-commodity advertising themes have two options. They can show how the commodity-based system can help improve customer profit by reducing costs, or they can show how the system can help improve customer profit by increasing customer sales. Sometimes a system can do both.

Improved return on investment can be implied or stated. Implication may be safer, but it is weaker. Quantification is far superior, even if customer cost savings or increased sales revenues must be estimated. The most effective approach is through case-history advertising, stating real improvements, such as the statement that Eastman Kodak makes about one of its microfilm customers: "Kodak showed us how to save $175,000 a year on order-entry options." In the case of another customer, individual file-search time is specified as having been reduced from hours to minutes with microfilm, resulting in a saving of $45,000 a year.

The IBM Model

For its computerized production-planning–program advertising, IBM references the Joseph Schlitz Brewing Company as a case history to promote the cost-reduction benefits of "packaging capacity studies which once took several weeks [and which] can now be done in 20 minutes." At Butterick Fashion Marketing Company, a division of American Can, manufacturing costs are reported to be cut by "half a million dollars with our online data base. Cash flow up 16%. Accounts receivable down 14%." For banks, IBM check-processing systems can improve profit by "increasing check-processing throughput by 30%." At Security Pacific Bank, "interactive computing helped increase net interest income by $127 million, or more than one-third." For customer companies in general, the

IBM System 7 is advertised as being able to improve profit by "reducing electricity bills by 10%."

In its advertising for the 3660 Supermarket System, a computer-assisted checkout counter, IBM promises two profit-improvement benefits: reduced costs and increased sales. IBM says to prospective supermarket customers, "We know where your operating costs cluster, and we can help you reduce them. For a store with gross weekly sales of $140,000, savings are projected at $7,651 a month by faster customer checkout and faster balancing of cash registers." The time required to check out an average order is reduced by almost 30 percent. In addition, the time and cost expenses of correcting checker errors are virtually eliminated. IBM estimates that its system can contribute potential savings of more than $91,000 per store annually.

There is more. Along with cost reductions, IBM also promises increased sales. IBM says to prospective supermarket customers, "We know why your customers buy, and we can help you stimulate them to buy even more." Based on the cost savings from the 3660 System, supermarkets can offer their customers greater numbers of advertised specials and deeper price cuts on specials. Customers also benefit from reduced checkout time. The combination of these benefits should add up to improved sales volume.

Use a separate copy of Planning Page 58 to work out your advertising promise to improve customer profit for each of your commodity products that you want to rebrand by system packaging. For every promise, document it with a genuine in-use case history or assume profit-improvement benefits from your own calculations.

PLANNING PAGES 43–58

PRODUCT-LINE LIFE-CYCLE ANALYSIS

Product line ______________________________

SIC #________ Industry classification ______________________

or consumer life-style ______________________

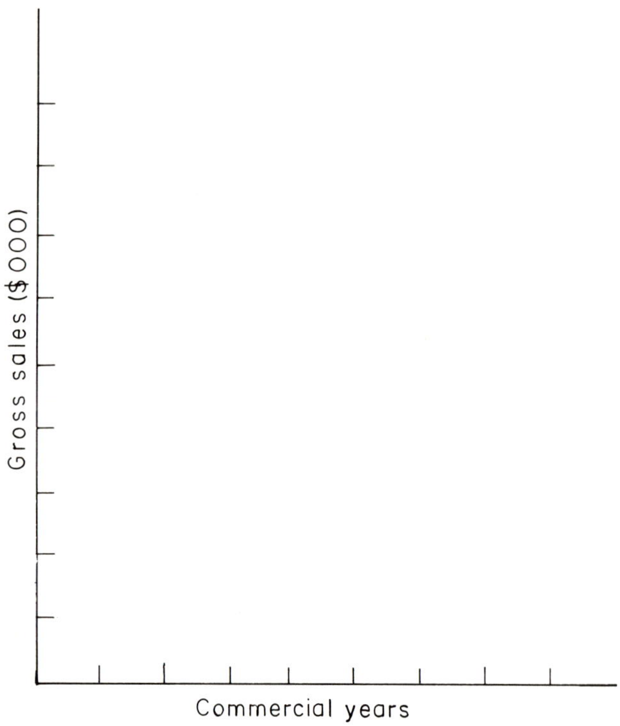

PRODUCT-LINE LIFE-CYCLE ANALYSIS

Product line ______________________________

SIC #______ Industry classification ______________________

or consumer life-style ______________________

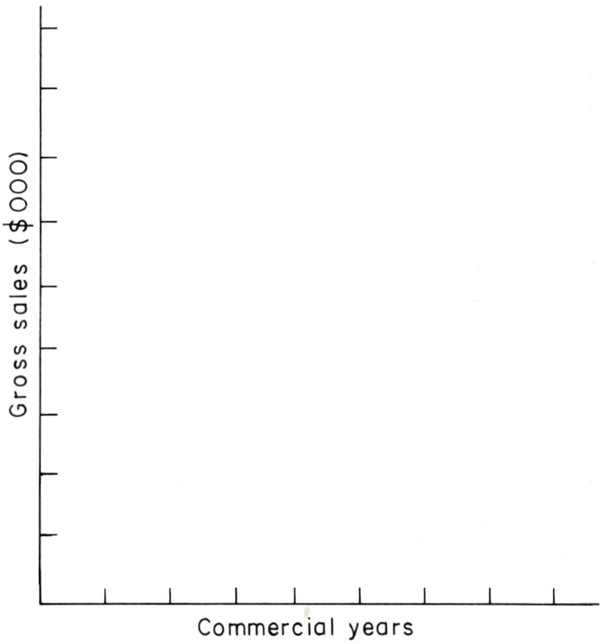

PRODUCT-LINE LIFE-CYCLE ANALYSIS

Product line ______________________________

SIC #______ Industry classification ______________________

or consumer life-style ______________________

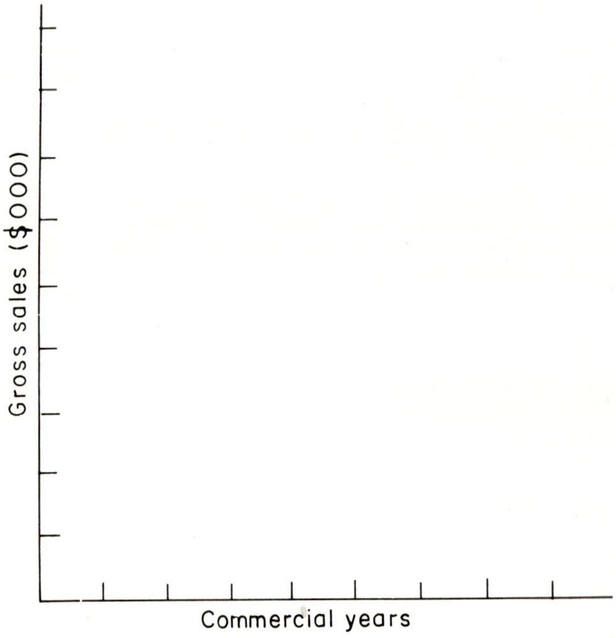

PRODUCT-LINE LIFE-CYCLE ANALYSIS

Product line ______________________________

SIC #______ Industry classification ______________________

or consumer life-style ______________________

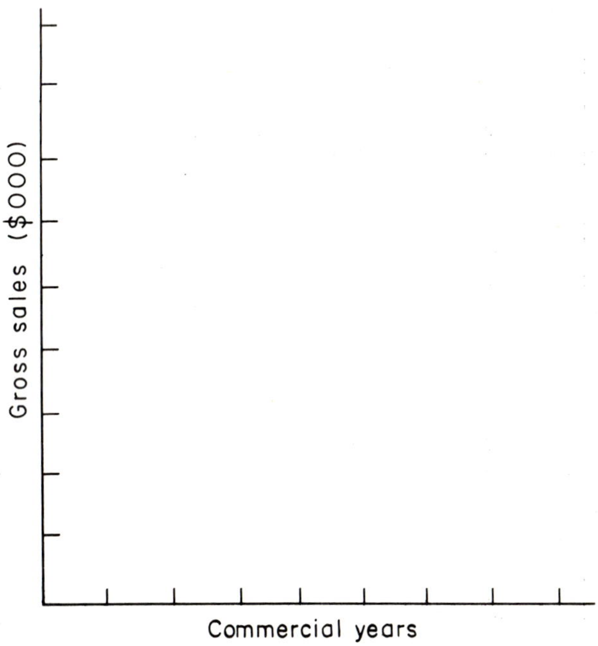

PRODUCT-LINE LIFE-CYCLE ANALYSIS

Product line ____

SIC #______ Industry classification ______________________

or consumer life-style ______________________

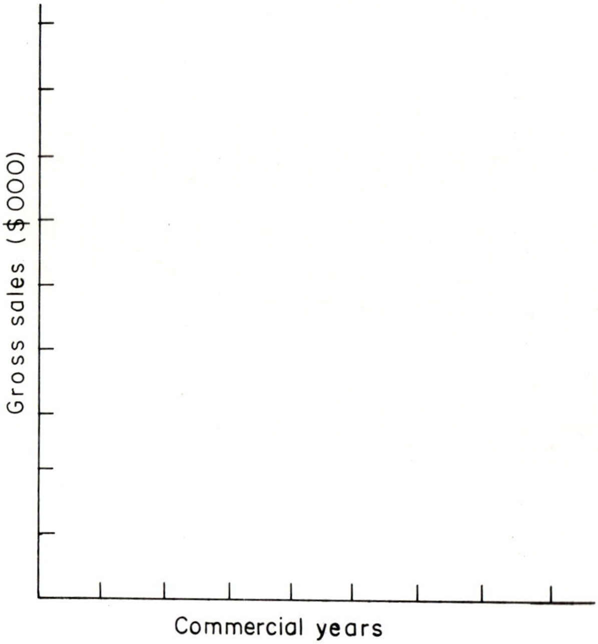

PRODUCT-REPOSITIONING STATEMENT

Product: ______________________________

SIC #______ Industry classification ______________

or consumer life-style ______________

1. As a result of ☐ Marketing renovation
   ☐ Technological renovation
   ☐ Both

   (Product) is now in position to preempt satisfaction of the heavy-profit-contributor market segment's single most crucial need for

   ____

2. To solve the market's major problem of (nature of problem and the operating process, function, or use pattern that it affects)

   ____

   ____

3. By applying the benefit(s) of:

   3.1. ______________________________

   3.2. ______________________________

   3.3. ______________________________

4. Which we deliver through (products, services, or systems):

   4.1. ______________________________

   4.2. ______________________________

   4.3. ______________________________

5. Derived from the technological capabilities of:

   5.1. ______________________________

   5.2. ______________________________

6. Marketed against the competition of:

Direct competition	Indirect competition
6.1. ______________	6.1. ______________
6.2. ______________	6.2. ______________
6.3. ______________	6.3. ______________

PRODUCT-REPOSITIONING STATEMENT

Product: ______________________________

SIC #______ Industry classification ______________________

or consumer life-style ______________________

1. As a result of ☐ Marketing renovation
   ☐ Technological renovation
   ☐ Both

   (Product) is now in position to preempt satisfaction of the heavy-profit-contributor market segment's single most crucial need for

   ____

2. To solve the market's major problem of (nature of problem and the operating process, function, or use pattern that it affects)

   ____

   ____

3. By applying the benefit(s) of:

   3.1. ______________________________

   3.2. ______________________________

   3.3. ______________________________

4. Which we deliver through (products, services, or systems):

   4.1. ______________________________

   4.2. ______________________________

   4.3. ______________________________

5. Derived from the technological capabilities of:

   5.1. ______________________________

   5.2. ______________________________

6. Marketed against the competition of:

Direct competition	Indirect competition
6.1. ______________	6.1. ______________
6.2. ______________	6.2. ______________
6.3. ______________	6.3. ______________

PRODUCT-REPOSITIONING STATEMENT

Product: ____________________

SIC #______ Industry classification ____________________

or consumer life-style ____________________

1. As a result of ☐ Marketing renovation
   ☐ Technological renovation
   ☐ Both

   (Product) is now in position to preempt satisfaction of the heavy-profit-contributor market segment's single most crucial need for

   ____

2. To solve the market's major problem of (nature of problem and the operating process, function, or use pattern that it affects)

   ____

   ____

3. By applying the benefit(s) of:

   3.1. ____________________

   3.2. ____________________

   3.3. ____________________

4. Which we deliver through (products, services, or systems):

   4.1. ____________________

   4.2. ____________________

   4.3. ____________________

5. Derived from the technological capabilities of:

   5.1. ____________________

   5.2. ____________________

6. Marketed against the competition of:

Direct competition	Indirect competition
6.1. ____________	6.1. ____________
6.2. ____________	6.2. ____________
6.3. ____________	6.3. ____________

PRODUCT-REPOSITIONING STATEMENT

Product: ______________________________

SIC #______ Industry classification ______________________________

or consumer life-style ______________________________

1. As a result of ☐ Marketing renovation
   ☐ Technological renovation
   ☐ Both

   (Product) is now in position to preempt satisfaction of the heavy-profit-contributor market segment's single most crucial need for

   ____

2. To solve the market's major problem of (nature of problem and the operating process, function, or use pattern that it affects) .

   ____

   ____

3. By applying the benefit(s) of:

   3.1. ______________________________

   3.2. ______________________________

   3.3. ______________________________

4. Which we deliver through (products, services, or systems):

   4.1. ______________________________

   4.2. ______________________________

   4.3. ______________________________

5. Derived from the technological capabilities of:

   5.1. ______________________________

   5.2. ______________________________

6. Marketed against the competition of:

Direct competition	Indirect competition
6.1. ____________	6.1. ____________
6.2. ____________	6.2. ____________
6.3. ____________	6.3. ____________

REBRANDED COMMODITY CASH-FLOW/PRICING STRATEGY CORRELATION

[Re]Brand __________ Sold to SIC #______ Industry classification ________

or consumer life-style ________

	Total year (19__)	First quarter	Second quarter	Third quarter	Fourth quarter
1. At price level of:					
$__,___/unit					
Most likely cash flow will be	$___,___,___*	$__,___,___	$__,___,___	$__,___,___	$__,___,___
Best-case cash flow could be	___,___,___	__,___,___	__,___,___	__,___,___	__,___,___
Worst-case cash flow could be	___,___,___	__,___,___	__,___,___	__,___,___	__,___,___
2. At price level of:					
$__,___/unit					
Most likely cash flow will be	$___,___,___	$__,___,___	$__,___,___	$__,___,___	$__,___,___
Best-case cash flow could be	___,___,___	__,___,___	__,___,___	__,___,___	__,___,___
Worst-case cash flow could be	___,___,___	__,___,___	__,___,___	__,___,___	__,___,___
3. At price level of:					
$__,___/unit					
Most likely cash flow will be	$___,___,___	$__,___,___	$__,___,___	$__,___,___	$__,___,___
Best-case cash flow could be	___,___,___	__,___,___	__,___,___	__,___,___	__,___,___
Worst case cash flow could be	___,___,___	__,___,___	__,___,___	__,___,___	__,___,___

* Common dollar value of 19__ as base year.

REBRANDED COMMODITY CASH-FLOW/PRICING STRATEGY CORRELATION

[Re]Brand ________ Sold to SIC #______ Industry classification ________
or consumer life-style ________

	Total year (19__)	First quarter	Second quarter	Third quarter	Fourth quarter
1. At price level of:					
$__,___/unit					
Most likely cash flow will be	$___,___,___*	$__,___,___	$__,___,___	$__,___,___	$__,___,___
Best-case cash flow could be	___,___,___	__,___,___	__,___,___	__,___,___	__,___,___
Worst-case cash flow could be	___,___,___	__,___,___	__,___,___	__,___,___	__,___,___
2. At price level of:					
$__,___/unit					
Most likely cash flow will be	$___,___,___	$__,___,___	$__,___,___	$__,___,___	$__,___,___
Best-case cash flow could be	___,___,___	__,___,___	__,___,___	__,___,___	__,___,___
Worst-case cash flow could be	___,___,___	__,___,___	__,___,___	__,___,___	__,___,___
3. At price level of:					
$__,___/unit					
Most likely cash flow will be	$___,___,___	$__,___,___	$__,___,___	$__,___,___	$__,___,___
Best-case cash flow could be	___,___,___	__,___,___	__,___,___	__,___,___	__,___,___
Worst case cash flow could be	___,___,___	__,___,___	__,___,___	__,___,___	__,___,___

* Common dollar value of 19__ as base year.

REBRANDED COMMODITY CASH-FLOW/PRICING STRATEGY CORRELATION

[Re]Brand ________ Sold to SIC #______ Industry classification ________
or consumer life-style ________

	Total year (19__)	First quarter	Second quarter	Third quarter	Fourth quarter
1. At price level of:					
$__,___/unit					
Most likely cash flow will be	$___,___,___*	$__,___,___	$__,___,___	$__,___,___	$__,___,___
Best-case cash flow could be	___,___,___	__,___,___	__,___,___	__,___,___	__,___,___
Worst-case cash flow could be	___,___,___	__,___,___	__,___,___	__,___,___	__,___,___
2. At price level of:					
$__,___/unit					
Most likely cash flow will be	$___,___,___	$__,___,___	$__,___,___	$__,___,___	$__,___,___
Best-case cash flow could be	___,___,___	__,___,___	__,___,___	__,___,___	__,___,___
Worst-case cash flow could be	___,___,___	__,___,___	__,___,___	__,___,___	__,___,___
3. At price level of:					
$__,___/unit					
Most likely cash flow will be	$___,___,___	$__,___,___	$__,___,___	$__,___,___	$__,___,___
Best-case cash flow could be	___,___,___	__,___,___	__,___,___	__,___,___	__,___,___
Worst case cash flow could be	___,___,___	__,___,___	__,___,___	__,___,___	__,___,___

* Common dollar value of 19__ as base year.

REBRANDED COMMODITY CASH-FLOW/PRICING STRATEGY CORRELATION

[Re]Brand ________ Sold to SIC #______ Industry classification ________
or consumer life-style ________

	Total year (19__)	First quarter	Second quarter	Third quarter	Fourth quarter
1. At price level of:					
$__,___/unit					
Most likely cash flow will be	$___,___,___*	$__,___,___	$__,___,___	$__,___,___	$__,___,___
Best-case cash flow could be	___,___,___	__,___,___	__,___,___	__,___,___	__,___,___
Worst-case cash flow could be	___,___,___	__,___,___	__,___,___	__,___,___	__,___,___
2. At price level of:					
$__,___/unit					
Most likely cash flow will be	$___,___,___	$__,___,___	$__,___,___	$__,___,___	$__,___,___
Best-case cash flow could be	___,___,___	__,___,___	__,___,___	__,___,___	__,___,___
Worst-case cash flow could be	___,___,___	__,___,___	__,___,___	__,___,___	__,___,___
3. At price level of:					
$__,___/unit					
Most likely cash flow will be	$___,___,___	$__,___,___	$__,___,___	$__,___,___	$__,___,___
Best-case cash flow could be	___,___,___	__,___,___	__,___,___	__,___,___	__,___,___
Worst case cash flow could be	___,___,___	__,___,___	__,___,___	__,___,___	__,___,___

* Common dollar value of 19__ as base year.

"TOO EXPENSIVE PRODUCT" SYSTEM PRESCRIPTION

To solve (customer problem and process): ____________________

____

System components:

1. ____

2. ____

3. ____

4. ____

5. ____

Cost to customer of perpetuating the problem	Price to customer for system solution	$ Benefit to customer from system use
$__,___,___	$__,___,___	$__,___,___

"COMPETITIVE-PARITY PRODUCT" SYSTEM PRESCRIPTION

To solve (customer problem and process): ______________________

____

System components:

1. ______________________________________

2. ______________________________________

3. ______________________________________

4. ______________________________________

5. ______________________________________

Cost to customer of perpetuating the problem	Price to customer for system solution	$ Benefit to customer from system use
$__,___,___	$__,___,___	$__,___,___

"RAPIDLY DEPRECIATING PRODUCT" SYSTEM PRESCRIPTION

To solve (customer problem and process): ____________________

____

System components:

1. ____________________________________

2. ____________________________________

3. ____________________________________

4. ____________________________________

5. ____________________________________

Cost to customer of perpetuating the problem	Price to customer for system solution	$ Benefit to customer from system use
$__,___,___	$__,___,___	$__,___,___

"TECHNOLOGICALLY OBSOLESCENT PRODUCT" SYSTEM PRESCRIPTION

To solve (customer problem and process): ______________________

____

System components:

1. ______________________________________

2. ______________________________________

3. ______________________________________

4. ______________________________________

5. ______________________________________

Cost to customer of perpetuating the problem	Price to customer for system solution	$ Benefit to customer from system use
$__,___,___	$__,___,___	$__,___,___

"FREQUENT-SERVICING PRODUCT" SYSTEM PRESCRIPTION

To solve (customer problem and process): ______________________

____

System components:

1. ____

2. ____

3. ____

4. ____

5. ____

Cost to customer of perpetuating the problem	Price to customer for system solution	$ Benefit to customer from system use
$__,___,___	$__,___,___	$__,___,___

"SOPHISTICATED-KNOWLEDGE PRODUCT" SYSTEM PRESCRIPTION

To solve (customer problem and process): ______________________

____

System components:

1. ____

2. ____

3. ____

4. ____

5. ____

Cost to customer of perpetuating the problem	Price to customer for system solution	$ Benefit to customer from system use
$__,___,___	$__,___,___	$__,___,___

SYSTEM CASH FLOW/PRICING STRATEGY CORRELATION

System: ________ Sold to (key-account customer) ________

	Total year (19__)	First quarter	Second quarter	Third quarter	Fourth quarter
1. At price level of:					
$__,___/system					
Based on ROI of __%					
Most likely cash flow will be	$___,___,___*	$__,___,___	$__,___,___	$__,___,___	$__,___,___
Best-case cash flow could be	___,___,___	__,___,___	__,___,___	__,___,___	__,___,___
Worst-case cash flow could be	___,___,___	__,___,___	__,___,___	__,___,___	__,___,___
2. At price level of:					
$__,___/system					
Based on ROI of __%					
Most likely cash flow will be	$___,___,___	$__,___,___	$__,___,___	$__,___,___	$__,___,___
Best-case cash flow could be	___,___,___	__,___,___	__,___,___	__,___,___	__,___,___
Worst-case cash flow could be	___,___,___	__,___,___	__,___,___	__,___,___	__,___,___
3. At price level of:					
$__,___/system					
Based on ROI of __%					
Most likely cash flow will be	$___,___,___	$__,___,___	$__,___,___	$__,___,___	$__,___,___
Best-case cash flow could be	___,___,___	__,___,___	__,___,___	__,___,___	__,___,___
Worst-case cash flow could be	___,___,___	__,___,___	__,___,___	__,___,___	__,___,___

* Common dollar value of 19__ as base year.

SYSTEM CASH FLOW/PRICING STRATEGY CORRELATION

System: ________ Sold to (key-account customer) ________

	Total year (19__)	First quarter	Second quarter	Third quarter	Fourth quarter
1. At price level of:					
$__,___/system					
Based on ROI of __%					
Most likely cash flow will be	$___,___,___*	$__,___,___	$__,___,___	$__,___,___	$__,___,___
Best-case cash flow could be	___,___,___	__,___,___	__,___,___	__,___,___	__,___,___
Worst-case cash flow could be	___,___,___	__,___,___	__,___,___	__,___,___	__,___,___
2. At price level of:					
$__,___/system					
Based on ROI of __%					
Most likely cash flow will be	$___,___,___	$__,___,___	$__,___,___	$__,___,___	$__,___,___
Best-case cash flow could be	___,___,___	__,___,___	__,___,___	__,___,___	__,___,___
Worst-case cash flow could be	___,___,___	__,___,___	__,___,___	__,___,___	__,___,___
3. At price level of:					
$__,___/system					
Based on ROI of __%					
Most likely cash flow will be	$___,___,___	$__,___,___	$__,___,___	$__,___,___	$__,___,___
Best-case cash flow could be	___,___,___	__,___,___	__,___,___	__,___,___	__,___,___
Worst-case cash flow could be	___,___,___	__,___,___	__,___,___	__,___,___	__,___,___

* Common dollar value of 19__ as base year.

SYSTEM CASH FLOW/PRICING STRATEGY CORRELATION

System: ________ Sold to (key-account customer) ________

	Total year (19__)	First quarter	Second quarter	Third quarter	Fourth quarter
1. At price level of:					
$__,___/system					
Based on ROI of __%					
Most likely cash flow will be	$___,___,___*	$__,___,___	$__,___,___	$__,___,___	$__,___,___
Best-case cash flow could be	___,___,___	__,___,___	__,___,___	__,___,___	__,___,___
Worst-case cash flow could be	___,___,___	__,___,___	__,___,___	__,___,___	__,___,___
2. At price level of:					
$__,___/system					
Based on ROI of __%					
Most likely cash flow will be	$___,___,___	$__,___,___	$__,___,___	$__,___,___	$__,___,___
Best-case cash flow could be	___,___,___	__,___,___	__,___,___	__,___,___	__,___,___
Worst-case cash flow could be	___,___,___	__,___,___	__,___,___	__,___,___	__,___,___
3. At price level of:					
$__,___/system					
Based on ROI of __%					
Most likely cash flow will be	$___,___,___	$__,___,___	$__,___,___	$__,___,___	$__,___,___
Best-case cash flow could be	___,___,___	__,___,___	__,___,___	__,___,___	__,___,___
Worst-case cash flow could be	___,___,___	__,___,___	__,___,___	__,___,___	__,___,___

* Common dollar value of 19__ as base year.

SYSTEM CASH FLOW/PRICING STRATEGY CORRELATION

System: ____________ Sold to (key-account customer) ____________

	Total year (19__)	First quarter	Second quarter	Third quarter	Fourth quarter
1. At price level of:					
$__,___/system					
Based on ROI of __%					
Most likely cash flow will be	$___,___,___*	$__,___,___	$__,___,___	$__,___,___	$__,___,___
Best-case cash flow could be	___,___,___	__,___,___	__,___,___	__,___,___	__,___,___
Worst-case cash flow could be	___,___,___	__,___,___	__,___,___	__,___,___	__,___,___
2. At price level of:					
$__,___/system					
Based on ROI of __%					
Most likely cash flow will be	$___,___,___	$__,___,___	$__,___,___	$__,___,___	$__,___,___
Best-case cash flow could be	___,___,___	__,___,___	__,___,___	__,___,___	__,___,___
Worst-case cash flow could be	___,___,___	__,___,___	__,___,___	__,___,___	__,___,___
3. At price level of:					
$__,___/system					
Based on ROI of __%					
Most likely cash flow will be	$___,___,___	$__,___,___	$__,___,___	$__,___,___	$__,___,___
Best-case cash flow could be	___,___,___	__,___,___	__,___,___	__,___,___	__,___,___
Worst-case cash flow could be	___,___,___	__,___,___	__,___,___	__,___,___	__,___,___

* Common dollar value of 19__ as base year.

MARKET VALUE INVENTORY MATRIX

SIC #_______ Industry classification ________________________

or consumer life-style ________________________

Change areas / Market values	Economic changes	Legis-lative changes	Market changes	Techno-logical changes	Compet-itive changes	Manage-ment changes	Labor force changes	Supply changes	Consum-erist changes
Business size and diversity									
Value/price relationship									
Service capability									
Distribution breadth; delivery capability									
Terms and conditions									
Technical sophistication									
Customer sensitivity									
Competitiveness									
Ethical posture									

MARKET VALUE ALIGNER

SIC #______ Industry classification ________________________

or consumer life-style _________________________

Market values	Required strategy to align business
1. Business size and diversity	1. ____________________
2. Value/price relationship	2. ____________________
3. Service capability	3. ____________________
4. Distribution breadth and delivery capability	4. ____________________
5. Terms and conditions	5. ____________________
6. Technical sophistication	6. ____________________
7. Customer sensitivity	7. ____________________
8. Competitiveness	8. ____________________
9. Ethical posture	9. ____________________

MARKET VALUE INVENTORY MATRIX

SIC #______ Industry classification ____________________

or consumer life-style ____________________

Change areas / Market values	Economic changes	Legis-lative changes	Market changes	Techno-logical changes	Compet-itive changes	Manage-ment changes	Labor force changes	Supply changes	Consum-erist changes
Business size and diversity									
Value/price relationship									
Service capability									
Distribution breadth; delivery capability									
Terms and conditions									
Technical sophistication									
Customer sensitivity									
Competitiveness									
Ethical posture									

MARKET VALUE ALIGNER

SIC #________ Industry classification ____________________________

or consumer life-style ____________________________

Market values	Required strategy to align business
1. Business size and diversity	1. ____________________________
2. Value/price relationship	2. ____________________________
3. Service capability	3. ____________________________
4. Distribution breadth and delivery capability	4. ____________________________
5. Terms and conditions	5. ____________________________
6. Technical sophistication	6. ____________________________
7. Customer sensitivity	7. ____________________________
8. Competitiveness	8. ____________________________
9. Ethical posture	9. ____________________________

MARKET VALUE INVENTORY MATRIX

SIC #______ Industry classification ____________________

or consumer life-style ____________________

Change areas / Market values	Economic changes	Legis-lative changes	Market changes	Techno-logical changes	Compet-itive changes	Manage-ment changes	Labor force changes	Supply changes	Consum-erist changes
Business size and diversity									
Value/price relationship									
Service capability									
Distribution breadth; delivery capability									
Terms and conditions									
Technical sophistication									
Customer sensitivity									
Competitiveness									
Ethical posture									

MARKET VALUE ALIGNER

SIC #______ Industry classification ____________________

or consumer life-style ____________________

Market values	Required strategy to align business
1. Business size and diversity	1. ________________
2. Value/price relationship	2. ________________
3. Service capability	3. ________________
4. Distribution breadth and delivery capability	4. ________________
5. Terms and conditions	5. ________________
6. Technical sophistication	6. ________________
7. Customer sensitivity	7. ________________
8. Competitiveness	8. ________________
9. Ethical posture	9. ________________

MARKET VALUE INVENTORY MATRIX

SIC #______ Industry classification ____________________

or consumer life-style ____________________

Change areas / Market values	Economic changes	Legis-lative changes	Market changes	Techno-logical changes	Compet-itive changes	Manage-ment changes	Labor force changes	Supply changes	Consum-erist changes
Business size and diversity									
Value/price relationship									
Service capability									
Distribution breadth; delivery capability									
Terms and conditions									
Technical sophistication									
Customer sensitivity									
Competitiveness									
Ethical posture									

MARKET VALUE ALIGNER

SIC #_______ Industry classification ____________________

or consumer life-style ____________________

Market values	Required strategy to align business
1. Business size and diversity	1. ____________________
2. Value/price relationship	2. ____________________
3. Service capability	3. ____________________
4. Distribution breadth and delivery capability	4. ____________________
5. Terms and conditions	5. ____________________
6. Technical sophistication	6. ____________________
7. Customer sensitivity	7. ____________________
8. Competitiveness	8. ____________________
9. Ethical posture	9. ____________________

KEY-INDUSTRY MARKETCENTERING PLAN

SIC #_____ Industry classification ________________

or consumer life-style ________________

	Systems to be sold to this market and components	Effects on decreasing customer cost clusters	Effects on increasing customer sales revenues	Average system cost	Average before-tax system rate of return
1.				$___,___,___	___%
2.				$___,___,___	___%
3.				$___,___,___	___%

KEY-INDUSTRY MARKETCENTERING PLAN

SIC #______ Industry classification ____________________

or consumer life-style ____________________

	Systems to be sold to this market and components	Effects on decreasing customer cost clusters	Effects on increasing customer sales revenues	Average system cost	Average before-tax system rate of return
1.				$---,---,---	---%
2.				$---,---,---	---%
3.				$---,---,---	---%

KEY-INDUSTRY MARKETCENTERING PLAN

SIC #______ Industry classification ______________________

or consumer life-style ______________________

	Systems to be sold to this market and components	Effects on decreasing customer cost clusters	Effects on increasing customer sales revenues	Average system cost	Average before-tax system rate of return
1.	________	________	________	$---,---,---	---%
	________	________	________		
	________	________	________		
	________	________	________		
2.	________	________	________	$---,---,---	---%
	________	________	________		
	________	________	________		
	________	________	________		
3.	________	________	________	$---,---,---	---%
	________	________	________		
	________	________	________		
	________	________	________		

BACKWARD INTEGRATION PLAN

To serve SIC #______ Industry classification _______________

or consumer life-style _______________

	Rate of return on investment		
Supply capability to be acquired or installed	(1) Total $ investment cost	(2) Average $ net income before taxes	Before-tax % rate of return; (2)÷(1)
1. ____________________	$__,___,___	$__,___,___	___%
2. ____________________	$__,___,___	$__,___,___	___%
3. ____________________	$__,___,___	$__,___,___	___%
4. ____________________	$__,___,___	$__,___,___	___%

BACKWARD INTEGRATION PLAN

To serve SIC #______ Industry classification ________________

or consumer life-style ________________

	Supply capability to be acquired or installed	Rate of return on investment		
		(1) Total \$ investment cost	(2) Average \$ net income before taxes	Before-tax % rate of return; (2)÷(1)
1.	____________________	\$__,___,___	\$__,___,___	___%
2.	____________________	\$__,___,___	\$__,___,___	___%
3.	____________________	\$__,___,___	\$__,___,___	___%
4.	____________________	\$__,___,___	\$__,___,___	___%

FORWARD INTEGRATION PLAN

To serve SIC ______ Industry classification ______________
or consumer life-style ______________

	Rate of return on investment		
End-user marketing capability to be acquired or installed	(1) Total $ investment cost	(2) Average $ net income before taxes	Before tax % rate of return; (2) ÷ (1)
1. ______________	$__,___,___	$__,___,___	___%
2. ______________	$__,___,___	$__,___,___	___%
3. ______________	$__,___,___	$__,___,___	___%
4. ______________	$__,___,___	$__,___,___	___%

FORWARD INTEGRATION PLAN

To serve SIC ______ Industry classification ________________
or consumer life-style ________________

	Rate of return on investment		
End-user marketing capability to be acquired or installed	(1) Total $ investment cost	(2) Average $ net income before taxes	Before tax % rate of return; (2) ÷ (1)
1. ________________	$__,___,___	$__,___,___	___%
2. ________________	$__,___,___	$__,___,___	___%
3. ________________	$__,___,___	$__,___,___	___%
4. ________________	$__,___,___	$__,___,___	___%

PROFIT-IMPROVEMENT ADVERTISING PLAN

Product: ______________________________

Advertised to (heavy-profit-contributor market): SIC #______ Industry classification ______

or consumer life-style ______

1. Advertising promise to improve customer profit by reducing customer costs
   (Specify exact cost cluster and dollar value of reduction)

   ____

   ____

   Case-history or test-stand documentation ______________________________

   ____

2. Advertising promise to improve customer profit by increasing customer sales revenues
   (Specify exact source of sales and dollar value of increase)

   ____

   ____

   Case-history or test-stand documentation ______________________________

   ____

PROFIT-IMPROVEMENT ADVERTISING PLAN

Product: ______________________________

Advertised to (heavy-profit-contributor market): SIC #______ Industry classification ________

or consumer life-style ________

1. Advertising promise to improve customer profit by reducing customer costs
   (Specify exact cost cluster and dollar value of reduction)

   ____

   ____

   Case-history or test-stand documentation ______________________________

   ____

2. Advertising promise to improve customer profit by increasing customer sales revenues
   (Specify exact source of sales and dollar value of increase)

   ____

   ____

   Case-history or test-stand documentation ______________________________

   ____

PROFIT-IMPROVEMENT ADVERTISING PLAN

Product: ______________________________

Advertised to (heavy-profit-contributor market): SIC #______ Industry classification ______

or consumer life-style ______

1. Advertising promise to improve customer profit by reducing customer costs
(Specify exact cost cluster and dollar value of reduction)

____

____

Case-history or test-stand documentation ______________________________

____

2. Advertising promise to improve customer profit by increasing customer sales revenues
(Specify exact source of sales and dollar value of increase)

____

____

Case-history or test-stand documentation ______________________________

____

6

PROFIT/COST-EFFICIENCY GRID

There are four basic options for brand building and commodity rebranding that trade off profit and cost efficiency:

1. 1.9 businesses and products that offer high profit probability and low cost efficiency.
2. 9.9 businesses and products that offer high profit probability and high cost efficiency.
3. 9.1 businesses and products that offer low profit probability and high cost efficiency.
4. 5.5 businesses and products that offer nominal profit probability and cost efficiency.

Accelerated growth, in keeping with all other business commitments, is a trade-off. Growth is expensive; there are no free lunches. Nor can you have your cake and eat it too. In the case of growing at an accelerated rate, profit is the cake. It is there for the making but only as a result of multiple trade-offs between cost and efficiency.

Some growth strategies are more profitable than others, but they tend to be less cost-efficient. Other growth strategies are more cost-efficient, but they tend to be less profitable. A couple of strategies are about equal in profitability and cost efficiency.

Exhibit 6-1 is a profit/cost-efficiency grid. It allows the principal options for brand building and commodity rebranding to be compared with each other. The grid's horizontal axis depicts the relative cost efficiency of six growth strategies. The vertical axis depicts their most likely profit probability. On each axis, the number 1 is the minimum, and the number 9 is the maximum. In positioning a strategy option, the horizontal axis number is given first as a reminder of the price of lunch.

The strategy positionings on the grid are intended to be useful generalizations. They are not to be interpreted precisely. Looked at in this way, five options can be fairly compared for profit probability and cost efficiency against a "base-case strategy" of deciding against accelerated growth and, instead, improving the cost efficiency of a mature-commodity business.

EXHIBIT 6-1

THE PROFIT/COST-EFFICIENCY GRID

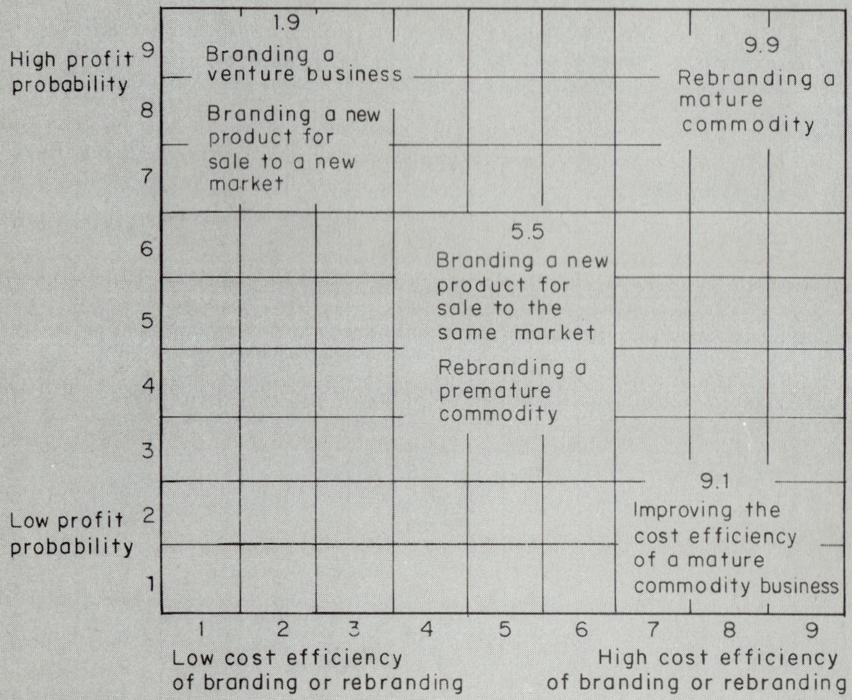

The base-case strategy is positioned at 9.1 on the grid. It is characterized by the probability of low profit, but it is almost always achievable at a relatively high cost efficiency because familiar and controllable functions are being managed in an improved manner for a familiar business that sells to a familiar market.

The rebranding of a mature commodity preserves most of these familiarities. Accordingly, it is also characterized by high cost efficiency. But, unlike a business in the 9.1 position, it can yield a high profit. It is therefore positioned on the grid at 9.9.

Brandable new products and premature commodities that are to be rebranded share some similar profit probabilities and cost efficiencies. This is due to the fact that a premature commodity undergoing rebranding appears to its market as a brandable new product. They are both positioned at 5.5 on the grid because they have a medium profit probability that can be achieved with moderate cost efficiency in familiar markets.

Two brand-building strategies share the highest risk/reward ratio. They are the branding of a new venture business and the branding of a new product for sale to a new market. In both cases, the profit probabilities and cost efficiencies are 180 degrees opposite the base case. With ventures and products of the new-market type, profit probability can be extremely high. Because so many unfamiliar variables must be planned for, coped with, monitored, and adjusted, the cost efficiency of building a branded venture business or a branded new product for sale to a new market can be very low. Whenever there is such a conjunction of unfamiliarities—an unfamiliar product or business matched with an unfamiliar market—this will be true.

Most businesses are 5.5 profit improvers. They settle for low-risk–low-reward increments. If a business is commodity-based, it is probably concentrating its growth planning at the 9.1 position. It can accrue new profits from increased sales. It can reduce old costs. It can introduce new operating efficiencies. But growth at an accelerated rate is improbable. To grow at a rate appreciably greater than GNP growth and greater than inflationary growth and growth in the cost of sales, new brands must be built or commodities repositioned into brands. To say the same thing in another way, growth in an accelerated manner cannot be accomplished merely by improving the management of internal functions or by a rearrangement of basic operating ratios. The market must be engaged.

This is the essential lesson of the profit/cost-efficiency grid. Substantial new profit, which is the ultimate criterion of growth, depends on strategies which build branded businesses or rebrand commodity businesses that offer preemptive benefits for new or newly emerging market needs. Accelerated growth comes from profitable new sales volume, not from cost reduction.

Growth that comes in significant increments has three relationships to markets: (1) it is market-targeted on a finite, solvable need; (2) it is market-centered to bring corporate resources to bear on market need in a dedicated, organized manner; and (3) it is market-derived. Small wonder, then, that marketing is the sole management tool that can deliver growth in the positions of high-profit probability.

PART THREE

POSTPLANNING

7

SELF-APPRAISING QUESTIONS

There are four postplanning questions for self-appraising growth plans:

1. Is commercial-growth positioning proprietary enough?
2. Is commercial-return potential high enough?
3. Are commercial driving forces optimally harnessed?
4. Are commercial assessment checkpoints properly programmed?

The market is the ultimate appraiser of all accelerated growth plans. Market judgment is final. In that sense, it is the only judgment that counts. Unfortunately, it generally comes too late to be corrected if it is negative. We therefore suggest that you conduct your own semifinal appraisal of the defensibility of your growth plan. There are four questions that you should ask yourself. They require you to support your plan's commercial-growth positioning, its commercial-return potential, the growth strategies that compose its driving forces, and the programming of its control checkpoints once the plan has been implemented.

Is My Plan's Commercial-Growth Positioning Proprietary Enough?

Commercial growth positioning is the basis for your marketing thrust. There are two considerations you should assess:

1. Is my growth positioning the best pairing I can make between my product's single most meaningful benefit and the single most meaningful need of its heavy-profit-contributor market?
2. Is my growth positioning the most differentiated I can make from competition?

Is My Plan's Commercial-Return Potential High Enough?

Commercial return is a managerial way of expressing return on investment. There are three considerations you should assess:

1. Is my incremental profit payoff sufficient to qualify my plan as an accelerated grower of internal capital?
2. Are my incremental costs of growth in line with maintaining tightfisted capital management practices, especially in regard to minimizing the enoughness of product quality?
3. Have I assumed as close to 100 percent probability as possible the worst-case impacts on profit, costs, and volume?

Are My Commercial Driving Forces Optimally Harnessed?

Commercial driving forces are your growth strategies. There are two considerations you should assess:

1. Do my growth strategies represent the minimal mix of brand-building and rebranding thrusts that I can make to achieve my maximum incremental growth objectives?
2. Are my incremental growth objectives the most meaningful I can make in terms of the strategies I have mixed?

Are My Commercial Assessment Checkpoints Properly Programmed?

Commercial checkpoints are your control stations. There are two considerations you should assess:

1. Is the staging of my checkpoints front-end–loaded toward the early phases of my plan's time frame so that I can solve small problems while they are still small and anticipate larger problems with sufficient early warning?
2. Have I tentatively identified the earliest checkpoint where I may have to revise the strategy of my plan, and do I have adequate foresight of the strategy revisions I will most likely be required to choose from?

These are tough questions. Use Planning Page 59 to summarize your answers in advance of every growth strategy thrust you commit. If your plan hangs tough in answer to the four self-appraisal questions, you will be able to go to market with increased confidence. Growth will not be preordained, but you will have reduced your risk and insured yourself against catastrophic failure. You will have made growth more graspable.

To make growth graspable is the function of accelerated growth planning. To grasp growth is the function of entrepreneurial management. The way to run a growing business is to put them both together. If you do, you may not necessarily have it made, but you will have made the growth mix, and that is the secret of being an accelerator of profit.

PLANNING PAGE
59

SELF-APPRAISAL CHECKLIST

1. Commercial-growth positioning

   ☐ 1.1. Single most meaningful product benefit paired with single most meaningful market need

   ☐ 1.2. Positioning most sharply differentiated from competition

2. Commercial-return potential

   ☐ 2.1. Incremental profit payoff sufficient to yield internal capital growth

   ☐ 2.2. Incremental costs minimized

   ☐ 2.3. Worst case estimated at least at 90 percent probability

3. Commercial driving forces

   ☐ 3.1. Growth strategies mixed minimally

   ☐ 3.2. Growth objectives most meaningful in relation to strategies

4. Commercial assessment checkpoints

   ☐ 4.1. Front-end-loaded

   ☐ 4.2. Earliest checkpoint for revising strategy identified as (date) __, 19__, by which time most likely strategy revisions will have been preplanned

APPENDIX 1

COMPENDIUM OF CAPITAL MANAGEMENT STRATEGIES

Growth profits are the source of internally generated capital. Unless you manage your capital resources well, capital will tend to leak out in cost-ineffective ways that can partially or completely nullify your achievements in new brand building or commodity rebranding. For this reason, we suggest that you improve the management of your capital appropriation strategies wherever necessary so that they can safeguard the value of the incremental capital you earn through accelerated growth.

There are two basic strategy systems for capital management. One is the management of *capital turnover.* The other is the management of *operating profit.*

Exhibit A-1 in Appendix 1 shows the major options that are open to you to improve capital turnover. The principal capital allocations you can affect are plant and equipment, inventories, receivables, and sales. By reducing the amount of funds invested in inventories, for example, you can reduce the total investment base of your business. As a result, you can improve your profit objective by reducing the cost of carrying inventory.

Exhibit A-2 shows the options that are open to you to improve operating profit. The principal capital allocations you can affect are cost of sales, selling expense, administrative expense, and sales. By increasing sales, for example, you can directly increase your operating profit and thereby improve your profit objective by earning new revenues.

Within the framework of these two strategy systems, there are six specific capital management strategies which we recommend that you control in conjunction with your growth planning:

1. Plant and equipment productivity improvement
2. Credit utilization improvement
3. Capital investment stretch-out
4. Past-investment recovery
5. Compliance-investment return improvement
6. Marginal-business turnaround

Plant and Equipment Productivity Improvement

New Plant, New Equipment, or Improved Operating Procedures

If you elect to plan improvement in your production capacity by adding new plant, refitting existing plant with new equipment, or implementing new operating procedures that will improve the cost effectiveness of utilizing your existing plant, use Planning Page 60 in Appendix 1. Work out the contribution to cost of your new plant, equipment, or procedures, the

EXHIBIT A-1

STRATEGY MIX FOR CAPITAL-TURNOVER IMPROVEMENT

SIC #______ Industry classification ________________________

or consumer life-style ________________________

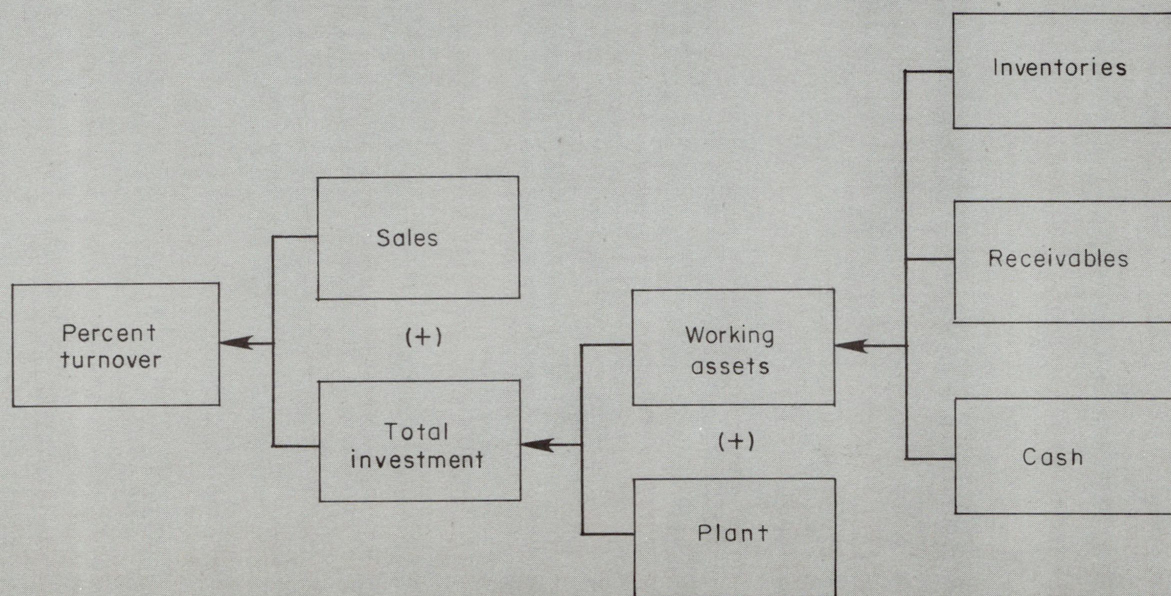

EXHIBIT A-2

STRATEGY MIX FOR OPERATING-PROFIT IMPROVEMENT

SIC #______ Industry classification ____________________

or consumer life-style ____________________

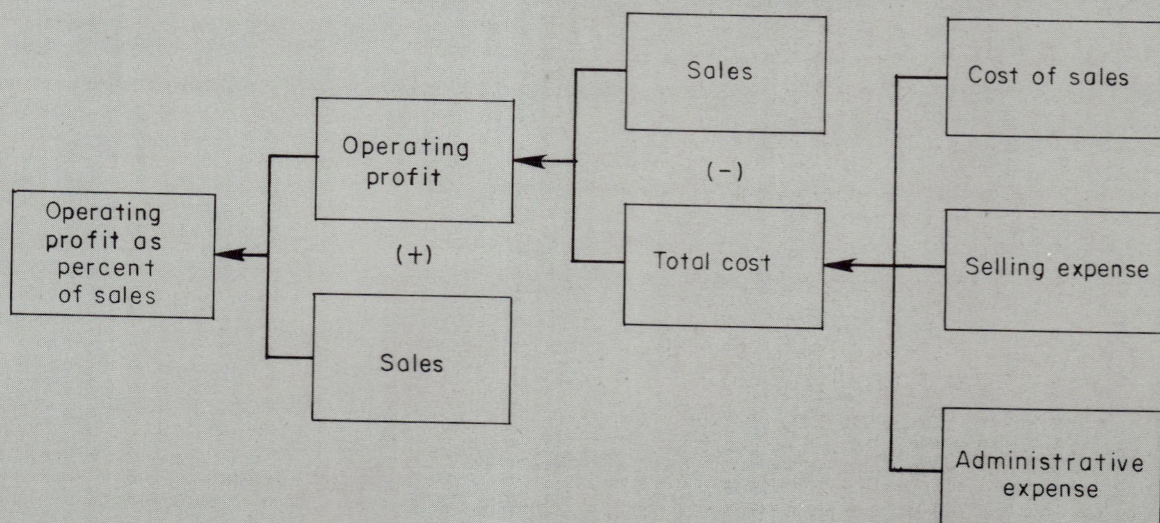

contribution to cost reduction or to increased unit output, and the return on invested capital you predict by Year 3.

Maintenance Improvement or Cost Reduction

If you elect to plan improvement in your maintenance or a reduction in its cost, use Planning Page 61. Work out the contribution to cost, the contribution to cost reduction or to increased unit output, and the return on invested capital you predict by Year 3.

Labor-Force-Use Improvement or Cost Reduction

If you elect to plan improvement in your labor force use or reduction in its cost, use Planning Page 62. Include contract renegotiation, automation, or employee motivation as both contributions to cost and contributions to cost reduction. Work out other contributions to cost, contributions to cost reduction or to increased unit output, and the return on invested capital you predict by Year 3.

Energy and Materials Use Improvement, Cost Reduction, or Source Substitution

If you elect to plan improvement in your energy use or reduction in its cost, use Planning Page 63. Work out the contribution to cost, the contribution to cost reduction or to increased unit output, and the return on invested capital you predict by Year 3. If the substitution of a new lower-cost energy source is part of your plan, use Planning Page 64 to describe the new source, the costs for its installation or conversion and for any employee retraining required to make it operational, the costs of assuring sufficient supply for at least 3 years following installation, and the total cost advantage that can accrue by Year 3.

If you elect to plan the substitution of one or more new materials, use Planning Page 65. Describe a substitute material in terms of its marketable benefits and deficits compared with the material being substituted for, the requirements for retooling and retraining imposed by the substitution, and its addition to or subtraction from cost. To estimate market acceptance of the substitute material before you commit yourself to change, use Planning Page 66 to forecast the degree of acceptance you can predict, the market's perceptions of the substitute material's assets and liabilities, and any alterations that the substitution will require in product positioning or price.

Manufacturing-Specification Consolidation

If you elect to plan the consolidation of manufacturing specifications in order to standardize one or more products, use Planning Page 67. Describe the specifications to be consolidated, the products to be standardized, and their contribution to cost reduction. Estimate the manufacturing and distribution costs to be saved. Include sales costs, advertising and sales promotion costs, and physical-distribution costs. Add any other costs that can be saved. Then estimate the probable sales loss, if any, resulting from your inability to supply the discontinued units.

Self-Manufacture

If you elect to make for yourself any ingredients, components, or packaging materials that you are currently purchasing from outside suppliers, use Planning Page 68. Describe the end product of your self-manufacture and estimate the cost savings you can achieve by Year 3. Also estimate a dollar value that can be assigned to the assurance of a reliable supply capability at a predictable cost. Then compare the value added by self-manufacture with the investment required for you to come on stream with your new capability and the rate of return you expect on the investment by Year 3.

Inventory Control Improvement

Inventory management has always been a compromise between too much and too little. An overinventoried position accumulates warehousing costs, incurs the risk of stockpiling stale and depreciating merchandise, and puts pressure on the sales force to move volume without regard for profit. It also encourages the loading of distribution channels and often acts to defeat retailer needs for profitable turnover. On the upside, an overinventoried situation can help ensure prompt customer service across a broad range of product models.

On the other hand, an underinventoried position creates out-of-stock conditions that can lose sales and distribution, sometimes for far longer periods of time than the temporary outage, discourage sales force motivation, cause waste circulation for advertising, and open the door to competitive entry into key accounts. On the upside, an underinventoried situation can reduce carrying costs and perhaps enable prices to be raised as long as merchandise is in short supply.

Many companies resolve this trade-off in favor of preferring to be safe rather than sorry. They deliberately maintain a slightly underinventoried position as a hedge against shifts in market demand or competitive innovation.

If you elect this cost-reduction strategy, you should make certain that you can step up production and distribution quickly in the event of increased demand or competitive threat. You will also have to assume at a high level of confidence that raw-material costs will not rise appreciably or that your access to suppliers will not significantly diminish while you remain underinventoried. Otherwise, you may be denied the ability to refill your pipelines on a price-competitive or profitable basis.

If you elect to plan improvement in your inventory control management, use Planning Page 69. Work out an optimal ratio between work in progress and finished goods for every major product. More work in progress means fewer finished goods in inventory. Enter the new unit levels of both categories of goods. Then work out the shortest possible interval between production and sales to optimize cash flow.

To quantify productivity improvement, you may elect to fix a quarterly percentage bench mark for one or more of the six strategies of improved plant and equipment productivity or improved maintenance, labor force use, energy and materials use, manufacturing-specification consolidation, and inventory control. If you do, use Planning Page 70 for every quarter's percentage fixing.

Credit Utilization Improvement

You can increase the effectiveness of your credit function by accelerating the collection of receivables and improving the creativity with which you help debtors make repayment. One of the acceleration strategies you can employ is to assess a monthly service fee for delinquent accounts. To help debtors, you may want to train your credit and collection staffs to consult with them about improving the profitability of their businesses.

You can lower the cost of your credit function by being more selective in allotting credit and by being more stringent in the sums you make available and the time frames you allow for payment. You can also train your sales force as well as your credit staff in reducing credit risk.

Use Planning Page 71 to plan the types and costs of the improvements you will budget for more cost-effective credit utilization, the debtors who will be affected, and the return on investment that you predict by Year 3.

Capital Investment Stretch-out

You can stretch out your capital investment schedule over a longer time frame to reduce its impact on your balance sheet. By deferring expansion, you may be able to apply your available capital resources to your highest-priority needs right now and still provide an emergency fund for contingencies. Under conditions of increasing inflation, you may also be able to invest softer dollars in the future than you can now. In a deflationary economy, every dollar will be able to buy more.

Some companies make it a regular operating practice to reserve capital for periodic long-term investments in breakthrough technologies. Procter & Gamble, IBM, Xerox, and Polaroid are examples. At P&G, for instance, sizable capital reserves have been committed to making quantum jumps in such diverse technologies as potato-chip manufacture, soap processing, and paper.

Use Planning Page 72 to plan the types and amounts of deferred capital investment you will make, the original and new commitment dates, and the dollar value of the deferred funds in terms of their probable value in the year in which you plan to release them.

Past-Investment Recovery

You can improve your capital position by recovering part or all of your investment in surplus assets by selling or scrapping them. You can also recover some of your initial capital expenditures by selling scrap, recycling it back into your operations, or selling by-products of your processes. Use Planning Page 73 to plan a surplus-asset sales strategy for scrap and by-products.

Compliance-Investment Return Improvement

You must safeguard your capital against undue cost ineffectiveness in the investments you make to meet compliance legislation affecting your environmental protection, the occupational safety and health of your staff, and your employment practices. Each of these investments represents a legislated cost. Each can represent a pure cost to you unless you can manage to achieve a return on your investment that will pay back some, most, or even all of the cost.

At the outset, legislated costs may appear to defy the prospect of any sort of return at all. Yet many companies are finding cost-balancing compensations. Some of the investment for environmental protection can often be returned through capture and sale of residual materials or recycling of control agents, marketing of consultation services in pollution control to companies with similar processes or problems, and achieving a measurable public relations effect through merchandising the news value of your community citizenship. Some investments for occupational safety and health as well as fair employment practices can be returned through achieving higher productivity, lower-cost risk management and reduced insurance liability, and an image-building value that can be translated into more cost-effective recruitment, improved labor relations, and favorable consideration by local, state, and federal legislatures.

Environmental Protection

Use Planning Page 74 to plan the types and amounts of air, water, or land pollution control that you will budget, the nature of the compliance legislation that will be satisfied, and the return on investment that you predict by Year 3.

Occupational Safety and Health

Use Planning Page 75 to plan the types and amounts of employee safety and health protection that you will budget, the nature of the compliance legislation that will be satisfied, and the return on investment that you predict by Year 3.

Equal Employment Opportunity

Use Planning Page 76 to plan the types and amounts of equal employment practices and procedures that you will budget, the nature of the compliance legislation that will be satisfied, and the return on investment that you predict by Year 3.

Marginal-Business Turnaround

Many marginal operations can be turned around into capital generators by reducing their cost base or increasing their profitable sales volume. Cost cutting can begin a turnaround, but you rarely can simply save your way to salvation. Sooner or later you must improve profits. If you elect to turn around a marginal business, use Planning Page 77 to work out a turnaround game plan. First work out the contribution to profit or loss and the contribution to cost made by the business last year and this year. Set turned-around objectives for next year. Then describe the strategies for cost reduction and sales improvement that you will employ in the form of a game plan to achieve your turned-around objectives. Use a separate copy of the planning page for every business you want to turn around in every market segment.

If turnaround does not appear to be operationally or financially feasible, you will have to consider divestment for a laggard division, department, product, or any other asset. There are two basic types of divestment. One is the sale of surplus assets, sometimes called "investment recovery." The other is the sale or write-off of entire businesses and product lines that have become surplus liabilities. This is sometimes called "smoothing."

There are six typical reasons for voluntarily considering a divestment strategy to achieve investment recovery or to accomplish smoothing:

1. Unsatisfactory profit performance or continuing loss
2. Debt reduction
3. Expansion needs that a parent company or a division is unable or unwilling to fulfill, especially if large development sums are required
4. Lack of top-management capability in a narrow or dishar-

monious line of business that is incompatible with the rest of the organization and interferes with management concentration on more successful operations

5. An earnings drain due to unsatisfactory performance and a desire to free financial and human resources for businesses that can offer greater opportunity for growth

6. Declining market opportunity or obsolescent technology

There are three considerations that may constrain divestment:

1. Repercussions on market share or distribution

2. Repercussions on manufacturing-cost allocation

3. Repercussions on internal morale or on the perceptions of the business community

To resolve these considerations, analyze the financial trade-off associated with each divestment candidate. Use Planning Page 78 to work out the estimated net proceeds from divestment. Also work out alternative investment opportunities for the net proceeds compared with the alternatives of continuing operations as is or of increasing investment to a profit-making level.

Divestment is a major marketing operation. It requires the application of skills in sales, law, finance, taxes and accounting, and industrial and public relations. Divestment should be targeted on potential purchasers who can make the best economic use of what they buy at a price based on value received.

An operating division may be sold in a single transaction, or it can be sold in parts. The sum of the parts may be greater in value than the whole. When a division is to be sold on the basis of its earning power, "extra assets" may be sold separately according to their asset value. These can include unused real estate, warehouses, and equipment. Extra assets often command prices well in excess of book value. If earnings on profitable products have been offset by losses on other products, it may be possible to separate the profitable operations of a business on an earning-power basis and sell the remaining extra assets on a specific-asset basis. Through independent sale, total realization can be significantly increased. Or, after analysis, it may be wise to retain the profitable operations and divest only the excess assets.

The selling price of a divestment should be optimistic. Purchasers buy a division's future, not its past. They generally evaluate most seriously the divestment's potential earnings and growth, perceived values beyond book value, cost savings that can be achieved under new management, and the capabilities of their key people to operate the divestment. These evaluations are tempered by fear that a competitor may make the purchase.

To make sales attractive to small buyers, several price-reducing strategies may be employed: selling off inventory in advance of disposal, financing receivables, mortgaging or arranging sale and leaseback of properties, and transferring tools and equipment to other units of the company.

Spin-off is a form of divestment that involves creating a subsidiary corporation to own a division or some specific assets. Shares in the subsidiary can be distributed proportionately to shareholders of the parent company or offered for public sale. Spin-off strategy lends itself to the disposal of any subsidiary capable of operating autonomously. Sometimes the very act of conferring autonomy on a spin-off will improve its earnings. If a spin-off is unable to attract market interest, liquidation is a logical alternative.

If you elect to divest, use a separate copy of Planning Page 79 to work out a divestment plan for every candidate in the market segments that will be affected. Use Planning Page 80 to work out a partial divestment plan.

Capital Control System

Capital management requires a comprehensive control system. The system should contain two elements. One is a capital control committee. The other is a quarterly review procedure for the committee.

In many companies, individual control functions are being merged into a central unit. The financial and operating control functions are coordinated at ITT. The Corning Glass Works has formed a master group to administer financial, planning, and production control activities. This type of master agency acts as a centralized general staff for control.

Permanent members of a control committee generally include representatives of three functions: finance, sales and marketing, and manufacturing. They meet on a monthly schedule to coordinate profit, cost, and volume relationships. Their objective is to keep costs in line with revenues, especially the cost of sales, to make sure that profit objectives are being supported by pricing and production, and to minimize inventory accumulation.

Representatives of other functions may sit in on the committee's meetings on an ad hoc basis, when and as needed. A frequent pair of resources are the research and development director and the director of market information and market research services. When materials shortages or inflated prices for materials can have a substantial effect on control, the purchasing director can also be an important adjunct to the control committee's decision making.

Use Planning Page 81 to organize a capital control committee and its ad hoc members. Then write a charter for the committee on Planning Page 82, giving it a set of objectives to be achieved and action directives for achieving them. Include in your directives the ability of the committee to recommend plant and equipment investment, improved maintenance or labor force use, the use of substitute or alternative energy sources and materials, inventory control, and other key coordinating and corrective allocations of resources that can affect productivity.

A capital control committee can be effective only if it meets at consistently short periodic intervals. For most companies, this is at least quarterly. At every review meeting, controls should be managed by exception. This means that only exceptions to planned performance are called to attention. The definition of an *exception* to planned performance is a *problem*. Planning Page 83 shows a model system for quarter-by-quarter exceptional control. Use it as an early-warning system to detect variances from budget in each market. Planning Page 84 should be correlated with your quarterly monitors on Planning Page 83. Use a separate copy of Planning Page 84 to define the problems causing variances in every market segment where they occur and recommend solution strategies for them.

Even quarterly control may not be frequent enough for some companies. In many businesses that sell through supermarkets and drug stores or that are heavily dependent on style or fad, 30 days has become the basic unit for exceptional-control review. In such cases, the quarter-by-quarter control system shown on Planning Page 83 must be foreshortened to a month-by-month system.

PLANNING PAGES
60–84

PRODUCTION CAPACITY IMPROVEMENT PLAN

Type and amount of capacity improvement	Contribution to cost	Contribution to cost reduction	Contribution to increased unit output	Return on investment by Year 3
1. New plant (specify market segments served and products)	$___,___,___	$__,___,___	#___,___,___	___% $__,___,___
SIC #_____: _______/_____				
SIC #_____: _______/_____				
SIC #_____: _______/_____				
SIC #_____: _______/_____				
2. New equipment (specify market segments served and products)	$___,___,___	$__,___,___	#___,___,___	___% $__,___,___
SIC #_____: _______/_____				
SIC #_____: _______/_____				
SIC #_____: _______/_____				
SIC #_____: _______/_____				
3. New operating procedures (Specify market segments served and products)	$___,___,___	$___,___,___	#___,___,___	___% $__,___,___
SIC #_____: _______/_____				
SIC #_____: _______/_____				
SIC #_____: _______/_____				
SIC #_____: _______/_____				

MAINTENANCE IMPROVEMENT OR COST-REDUCTION PLAN

Maintenance improvement and/or cost-reduction strategy	Contribution to cost	Contribution to cost reduction	Contribution to increased unit output	Return on investment by Year 3
1. ____________	$__,___,___	$__,___,___	#___,___,___	___% $__,___,___
2. ____________	$__,___,___	$__,___,___	#___,___,___	___% $__,___,___
3. ____________	$__,___,___	$__,___,___	#___,___,___	___% $__,___,___

LABOR FORCE USE IMPROVEMENT OR COST-REDUCTION PLAN

Labor force use improvement and/or cost-reduction strategy	Contribution to cost	Contribution to cost reduction	Contribution to increased unit output	Return on investment by Year 3
1. ______________________	$--,---,---	$--,---,---	#---,---,---	---%
				$--,---,---
2. ______________________	$--,---,---	$--,---,---	#---,---,---	---%
				$--,---,---
3. ______________________	$--,---,---	$--,---,---	#---,---,---	---%
				$--,---,---

ENERGY USE IMPROVEMENT OR COST-REDUCTION PLAN

Energy use improvement and/or cost-reduction strategy	Contribution to cost	Contribution to cost reduction	Contribution to increased unit output	Return on investment by Year 3
1. ________________	$__,___,___	$__,___,___	#___,___,___	___% $__,___,___
2. ________________	$__,___,___	$__,___,___	#___,___,___	___% $__,___,___
3. ________________	$__,___,___	$__,___,___	#___,___,___	___% $__,___,___

ENERGY SOURCE SUBSTITUTION PLAN

☒ Old source and new source ☑	Total cost for installation, conversion, and retraining	Total cost for assuring sufficient supply through Year 3 (19__)	Total cost advantage or disadvantage by Year 3 (19__)
☐ Electricity ☐	$__,___,___	$__,___,___	+/− $__,___,___
☐ Natural gas ☐	$__,___,___	$__,___,___	+/− $__,___,___
☐ Oil ☐	$__,___,___	$__,___,___	+/− $__,___,___
☐ Coal ☐	$__,___,___	$__,___,___	+/− $__,___,___
☐ Solar ☐	$__,___,___	$__,___,___	+/− $__,___,___

MATERIALS SUBSTITUTION PLAN

Substitute material and material substituted for	Marketable benefits or deficits of substitute material	Requirements: Retool	Requirements: Retrain	Addition to or Subtraction from cost
1. ________	Benefits:			+/– $__,___,___
________	________	________	________	
	________	________	________	
	________	________	________	
	________	________	________	
	Deficits:			
	________			
	________			
2. ________	Benefits:			+/– $__,___,___
________	________	________	________	
	________	________	________	
	________	________	________	
	________	________	________	
	Deficits:			
	________			
	________			

SUBSTITUTE-MATERIAL MARKET ACCEPTANCE ESTIMATE

Material: ______________________________

Market segment	Perceived assets and liabilities	Our products in which used and required changes in their positioning or price
SIC #______	Assets:	Product: ______________
Industry classification ______	______________________	Position or price change:
or customer life-style ______	______________________	______________________
	______________________	______________________
	Liabilities:	______________________
	______________________	+/- $___/unit
	______________________	
SIC #______	Assets:	Product: ______________
Industry classification ______	______________________	Position or price change:
or customer life-style ______	______________________	______________________
	______________________	______________________
	Liabilities:	______________________
	______________________	+/- $___/unit
	______________________	

MANUFACTURING-SPECIFICATION CONSOLIDATION PLAN

Product line: ____

	Old specifications and new consolidated specifications	Products to be standardized	Costs to be saved: Manufacturing	Costs to be saved: Distribution	Costs to be saved: ________ (Other)	Estimated $ sales lost
1.	______________/	________________	$__,___,___	$__,___,___	$__,___,___	$__,___,___
	________________	________________				
		________________				
2.	______________/	________________	$__,___,___	$__,___,___	$__,___,___	$__,___,___
	________________	________________				
		________________				
3.	______________/	________________	$__,___,___	$__,___,___	$__,___,___	$__,___,___
	________________	________________				
		________________				

SELF-MANUFACTURE PLAN

Ingredient, component, or packaging for self-manufacture	Value added by self-manufacture: Projected cost savings by Year 3	Value added by self-manufacture: Estimated $ value of assured supply	Investment required to come on stream	Return on investment by Year 3
1. ____________	$--,---,---	$--,---,---	$---,---,---	$--,---,---
				---%
2. ____________	$--,---,---	$--,---,---	$---,---,---	$--,---,---
				---%
3. ____________	$--,---,---	$--,---,---	$---,---,---	$--,---,---
				---%

INVENTORY CONTROL PLAN

Products	Optimal ratio between work in progress and finished goods	New unit levels: New unit level of work in progress	New unit levels: New unit level of finished goods	New interval between production and sale
1. ____________	__/__	#___,___,___	#___,___,___	___ days
2. ____________	__/__	#___,___,___	#___,___,___	___ days
3. ____________	__/__	#___,___,___	#___,___,___	___ days
4. ____________	__/__	#___,___,___	#___,___,___	___ days
5. ____________	__/__	#___,___,___	#___,___,___	___ days
6. ____________	__/__	#___,___,___	#___,___,___	___ days

PRODUCTIVITY IMPROVEMENT BENCH-MARK PLAN

For the Year 19__

Operations to be applied to	% productivity improvement bench marks to be enforced for ensuring capital formation			
	Quarter 1	Quarter 2	Quarter 3	Quarter 4
1. Plant and equipment	---	---	---	---
2. Maintenance	---	---	---	---
3. Labor force use	---	---	---	---
4. Energy and materials	---	---	---	---
5. Manufacturing specifications	---	---	---	---
6. Inventory control				

PRODUCTIVITY IMPROVEMENT BENCH-MARK PLAN

For the Year 19__

Operations to be applied to	% productivity improvement bench marks to be enforced for ensuring capital formation			
	Quarter 1	Quarter 2	Quarter 3	Quarter 4
1. Plant and equipment	___	___	___	___
2. Maintenance	___	___	___	___
3. Labor force use	___	___	___	___
4. Energy and materials	___	___	___	___
5. Manufacturing specifications	___	___	___	___
6. Inventory control	___	___	___	___

PRODUCTIVITY IMPROVEMENT BENCH-MARK PLAN

For the Year 19__

Operations to be applied to	% productivity improvement bench marks to be enforced for ensuring capital formation			
	Quarter 1	Quarter 2	Quarter 3	Quarter 4
1. Plant and equipment	___	___	___	___
2. Maintenance	___	___	___	___
3. Labor force use	___	___	___	___
4. Energy and materials	___	___	___	___
5. Manufacturing specifications	___	___	___	___
6. Inventory control				

PRODUCTIVITY IMPROVEMENT BENCH-MARK PLAN

For the Year 19__

Operations to be applied to	% productivity improvement bench marks to be enforced for ensuring capital formation			
	Quarter 1	Quarter 2	Quarter 3	Quarter 4
1. Plant and equipment	___	___	___	___
2. Maintenance	___	___	___	___
3. Labor force use	___	___	___	___
4. Energy and materials	___	___	___	___
5. Manufacturing specifications	___	___	___	___
6. Inventory control	___	___	___	___

CREDIT UTILIZATION IMPROVEMENT PLAN

Types and $ costs of improvement	Classifications of debtors affected	$ and % return on investment by Year 3
1. To increase effectiveness		
1.1. ________	________	$___,___,___/___% ROI
$___,___,___	________	
1.2. ________	________	$___,___,___/___% ROI
$___,___,___	________	
1.3. ________	________	$___,___,___/___% ROI
$___,___,___	________	
2. To reduce costs		
2.1. ________	________	$___,___,___/___% ROI
$___,___,___	________	
2.2. ________	________	$___,___,___/___% ROI
$___,___,___	________	
2.3. ________	________	$___,___,___/___% ROI
$___,___,___	________	

CAPITAL INVESTMENT STRETCH-OUT PLAN

	Types and $ amounts of deferred investment	Original and new commitment dates	Most likely $ value of funds when released in 19__
1.	________________ $___,___,___	________19__/________19__	$___,___,___
2.	________________ $___,___,___	________19__/________19__	$___,___,___
3.	________________ $___,___,___	________19__/________19__	$___,___,___
4.	________________ $___,___,___	________19__/________19__	$___,___,___

PAST-INVESTMENT RECOVERY PLAN

Type of surplus asset	Fair market value	$ value of recovery strategy		
		Sell as scrap	Sell as by-product	Recycle
1. ____________________	$___,___,___	$___,___	$___,___,___	$___,___
2. ____________________	$___,___,___	$___,___	$___,___,___	$___,___
3. ____________________	$___,___,___	$___,___	$___,___,___	$___,___
4. ____________________	$___,___,___	$___,___	$___,___,___	$___,___
5. ____________________	$___,___,___	$___,___	$___,___,___	$___,___

ENVIRONMENTAL PROTECTION INVESTMENT PLAN

	Types and $ amounts of investment	Compliance legislation satisfied	$ and % return on investment by Year 3
1.	______________________ $___,___,___	______________________	$___,___,___/___% ROI
2.	______________________ $___,___,___	______________________	$___,___,___/___% ROI
3.	______________________ $___,___,___	______________________	$___,___,___/___% ROI
4.	______________________ $___,___,___	______________________	$___,___,___/___% ROI

OCCUPATIONAL SAFETY AND HEALTH INVESTMENT PLAN

Types and $ amounts of investment	Compliance legislation satisfied	$ and % return on investment by Year 3
1. ________ $___,___,___	________	$___,___,___/___% ROI
2. ________ $___,___,___	________	$___,___,___/___% ROI
3. ________ $___,___,___	________	$___,___,___/___% ROI
4. ________ $___,___,___	________	$___,___,___/___% ROI

EQUAL EMPLOYMENT OPPORTUNITY INVESTMENT PLAN

	Types and $ amounts of investment	Compliance legislation satisfied	$ and % return on investment by Year 3
1.	________ $___,___,___	________	$___,___,___/___% ROI
2.	________ $___,___,___	________	$___,___,___/___% ROI
3.	________ $___,___,___	________	$___,___,___/___% ROI
4.	________ $___,___,___	________	$___,___,___/___% ROI

MARGINAL BUSINESS TURNAROUND PLAN

Business: ______________________________

SIC #______ Industry classification ______________

or consumer life-style ______________

	Next year (19__) turned around to	From this year (19__) budgeted	Last year (19__) actual
Contribution to profit or loss	$__,___,___	$__,___,___	$__,___,___
Contribution to cost	$__,___,___	$__,___,___	$__,___,___

Turnaround game plan

____

____

____

____

____

____

____

____

DIVESTMENT CANDIDATE ANALYSIS

Division or department: ________________________________

SIC #______ Industry classification ____________________

or consumer life-style ____________________

If retained		If divested	
Estimated net proceeds from continued use	Estimated extra net proceeds or estimated extra net investment to make profitable	Estimated net proceeds from divestment	If reinvested, estimated ROI and net proceeds from alternative opportunities
$___,___,___	$___,___,___	$___,___,___	1. Opportunity: ________ ________ ROI: ___% $___,___,___
			2. Opportunity: ________ ________ ROI: ___% $___,___,___

DIVESTMENT PLAN

Division or Department: ______________________

SIC #______ Industry classification ______________

or consumer life-style ______________

Book value	Estimated net proceeds based on sales price at __ × earnings	Estimated total cost of divestment	Estimated net proceeds or cost for reinvestment	ROI from, and type of, alternative investment opportunities
\$___,___,___	\$___,___,___	\$___,___,___	\$___,___,___	1. Opportunity:
			Proceeds =	______________
			\$___,___,___	______________
			(minus) Cost =	ROI: ___%
			\$___,___,___	2. Opportunity:
				______________
				______________
				ROI: ___%

DIVESTMENT PLAN

Division or Department: ____________________

SIC #______ Industry classification ____________________

or consumer life-style ____________________

Book value	Estimated net proceeds based on sales price at __ × earnings	Estimated total cost of divestment	Estimated net proceeds or cost for reinvestment	ROI from, and type of, alternative investment opportunities
$___,___,___	$___,___,___	$___,___,___	$___,___,___	1. Opportunity:
			Proceeds =	____________________
			$___,___,___	____________________
			(minus) Cost =	ROI: ___%
			$___,___,___	
				2. Opportunity:
				____________________
				____________________
				ROI: ___%

PARTIAL DIVESTMENT PLAN

Division or department: ____________________

SIC #______ Industry classification ____________________

or consumer life-style ____________________

Itemization of excess assets

1. ____________________	5. ____________________
2. ____________________	6. ____________________
3. ____________________	7. ____________________
4. ____________________	8. ____________________

Book value	Estimated net proceeds based on sales price at __ × earnings	Estimated total cost of divestment	Estimated net proceeds or cost for reinvestment
$___,___,___	$___,___,___	$___,___,___	$___,___,___

Proceeds =

$___,___,___

(minus)
Cost =

$___,___,___

CAPITAL CONTROL COMMITTEE

	Financial control	Sales and marketing control	Manufacturing control
Name:	______________	______________	______________
Title:	______________	______________	______________

AD HOC MEMBERS

	______________ (Function)	______________ (Function)	______________ (Function)
Name:	______________	______________	______________
Title:	______________	______________	______________

CAPITAL CONTROL COMMITTEE CHARTER

The Capital Control Committee is chartered to:

To achieve these objectives, the committee will:

QUARTERLY MONITOR

Quarter 1 2 3 4 19__

Planned quarterly objectives	Actual performance	+/− variances (000)	Decision #
1. Plant and equipment investment (including environmental protection)			
$___,___,___	$___,___,___	+/− $___,___	1 2 3
2. Maintenance investment			
$___,___,___	$___,___,___	+/− $___,___	1 2 3
3. Labor force investment			
$___,___,___	$___,___,___	+/− $___,___	1 2 3
4. Energy and materials investment			
$___,___,___	$___,___,___	+/− $___,___	1 2 3
5. Inventory investment			
$___,___,___	$___,___,___	+/− $___,___	1 2 3

> Decision 1 is a green flag. Go full speed ahead. Decision 2 is a yellow flag. Proceed with caution. Decision 3 is a red flag. Take corrective action before proceeding further. If you make Decision 3, alter your growth plan's objectives and strategies.

QUARTERLY MONITOR

Quarter 1 2 3 4 19__

	Planned quarterly objectives	Actual performance	+/– variances (000)	Decision #
1. Plant and equipment investment (including environmental protection)				
	$___,___,___	$___,___,___	+/– $___,___	1 2 3
2. Maintenance investment				
	$___,___,___	$___,___,___	+/– $___,___	1 2 3
3. Labor force investment				
	$___,___,___	$___,___,___	+/– $___,___	1 2 3
4. Energy and materials investment				
	$___,___,___	$___,___,___	+/– $___,___	1 2 3
5. Inventory investment				
	$___,___,___	$___,___,___	+/– $___,___	1 2 3

Decision 1 is a green flag. Go full speed ahead. Decision 2 is a yellow flag. Proceed with caution. Decision 3 is a red flag. Take corrective action before proceeding further. If you make Decision 3, alter your growth plan's objectives and strategies.

QUARTERLY MONITOR

Quarter 1 2 3 4 19__

Planned quarterly objectives	Actual performance	+/- variances (000)	Decision #
1. Plant and equipment investment (including environmental protection)			
$___,___,___	$___,___,___	+/- $___,___	1 2 3
2. Maintenance investment			
$___,___,___	$___,___,___	+/- $___,___	1 2 3
3. Labor force investment			
$___,___,___	$___,___,___	+/- $___,___	1 2 3
4. Energy and materials investment			
$___,___,___	$___,___,___	+/- $___,___	1 2 3
5. Inventory investment			
$___,___,___	$___,___,___	+/- $___,___	1 2 3

Decision 1 is a green flag. Go full speed ahead. Decision 2 is a yellow flag. Proceed with caution. Decision 3 is a red flag. Take corrective action before proceeding further. If you make Decision 3, alter your growth plan's objectives and strategies.

QUARTERLY MONITOR

Quarter 1 2 3 4 19__

	Planned quarterly objectives	Actual performance	+/- variances (000)	Decision #
1. Plant and equipment investment (including environmental protection)				
	$___,___,___	$___,___,___	+/- $___,___	1 2 3
2. Maintenance investment				
	$___,___,___	$___,___,___	+/- $___,___	1 2 3
3. Labor force investment				
	$___,___,___	$___,___,___	+/- $___,___	1 2 3
4. Energy and materials investment				
	$___,___,___	$___,___,___	+/- $___,___	1 2 3
5. Inventory investment				
	$___,___,___	$___,___,___	+/- $___,___	1 2 3

Decision 1 is a green flag. Go full speed ahead. Decision 2 is a yellow flag. Proceed with caution. Decision 3 is a red flag. Take corrective action before proceeding further. If you make Decision 3, alter your growth plan's objectives and strategies.

PROBLEM DEFINITION AND SOLUTION STRATEGY RECOMMENDATION

SIC #______ Industry classification ____________________

or consumer life-style ____________________

Problem definition

Recommended solution strategy, elapsed time, and projected remedial effect on variance

PROBLEM DEFINITION AND SOLUTION STRATEGY RECOMMENDATION

SIC #______ Industry classification ____________________

or consumer life-style ____________________

Problem definition

____

____

____

Recommended solution strategy, elapsed time, and projected remedial effect on variance

____

____

____

____

____

PROBLEM DEFINITION AND SOLUTION STRATEGY RECOMMENDATION

SIC #______ Industry classification ____________________

or consumer life-style ____________________

Problem definition

Recommended solution strategy, elapsed time, and projected remedial effect on variance

PROBLEM DEFINITION AND SOLUTION STRATEGY RECOMMENDATION

SIC #________ Industry classification ______________________________

or consumer life-style ________________________________

Problem definition

____

____

____

Recommended solution strategy, elapsed time, and projected remedial effect on variance

____

____

____

____

____

APPENDIX 2

ACCELERATED GROWTH PLAN TITLE PAGES

ACCELERATED GROWTH PLAN
for

____

(Business name)

Responsive to the __19__/__19__ Business Environment

CONTENTS

1

GROWTH MARKET TARGET AND FAIR ASSUMPTIONS

2

GROWTH SOURCES AND OBJECTIVES

3

BRAND-BUILDING STRATEGY THRUST

4

REBRANDING STRATEGY THRUST

INDEX